Under His Wings

Under His
Wings

*How Faith on the Front Lines
Has Protected American Troops*

EMILY COMPAGNO

WEEK ENDING JULY 19, 1930

Liberty

A Weekly for Everybody

5¢

OVER 2,250,000 NET PAID CIRCULATION

Marianthe Once Again

BRENNAN ~ CHADWICK ~ WINSLOW ~ BENCHLEY ~ DOHER

FOR MY PARENTS

*My strong, inspiring mother, whose encouragement has known
no bounds, and whose loving dedication and meticulous research as a
collector of stories has blessed generations of families, especially ours.*

*And my father, whose steadfast service and honor continue
well beyond the commander's uniform, and whose unfailing
love and leadership have guided me to where I am today.*

The two of you gave me wings. I'm so proud to be your daughter.

I love you both.

Whoever dwells in the shelter of the Most High

will rest in the shadow of the Almighty.

I will say of the Lord, "He is my refuge and my fortress,

my God, in whom I trust."

Surely He will save you

from the fowler's snare

and from the deadly pestilence.

He will cover you with His feathers,

and under His wings you will find refuge;

His faithfulness will be your shield and rampart.

You will not fear the terror of night,

nor the arrow that flies by day,

nor the pestilence that stalks in the darkness,

nor the plague that destroys at midday.

A thousand may fall at your side,

ten thousand at your right hand,

but it will not come near you.

—PSALM 91

Contents

Under His Wings

INTRODUCTION

History books chronicle the ferocity of war; portraying the details of battles; describing successes and failures and close calls; setting forth the courageous and honorable actions by soldiers who exceed duty and secure freedom in the thick of combat. But what those black-and-white details don't reveal is the unseen force at work: the origin of tide-turning courage, the source of the invisible protection, the embrace in which the soldier found comfort. Historians may question: In the depths of fear and despair, amid the brutality of violence, in the throes of pain, and in the moments of jubilation, Who do soldiers turn to? Who protects them? The saved know.

It is the Lord Who goes before us, Who is always with us, Who will never leave or forsake us. From Samson using the mere jawbone of a donkey to slay a thousand men to a simple slingshot equipping David to overcome Goliath, the Bible is replete with examples of His faithfulness shielding soldiers in battle. Yet Jesus Christ is the same yesterday, today, and forever.

The warriors in this book each experienced intimate connections with God on the battlefield. The stories within reveal the most profoundly life-changing moments soldiers had while serving on the front lines: a Green Beret heard God's voice in the middle of a firefight in Iraq; an infantryman felt His direction during an ambush in the jungles of Vietnam; a Ranger realized His calling on a tarmac in Mogadishu; a prisoner of war had his prayers answered during torture sessions. Firsthand, riveting accounts of God by the side and in the hearts of soldiers, getting them through torture, pain, despair, separation, fear, anger, and grief. Through prayer, through miracles, through interactions with angels, these remind us "What is impossible with man, is possible with God" (Luke 18:27).

There is joy in these memories too. Deeply touching accounts of rejoice and worship in the unlikeliest of circumstances, reverence within the humblest settings. God promises us He will strengthen us and help us, uphold us with His righteous hand. These warriors' souls are saved, their spirits cared for.

Some of these accounts are personal to me. My family's extensive military service has left imprints all over the world, with my relatives fighting overseas and far away in past wars and conflicts and up through modern history, from Italy and England to France and Germany, from the Pacific Theater and the Philippines all the way to Afghanistan and Iraq. My blood carries the blood of those in my family who died on European battlefields like Flanders Fields and the Russian Front, and of those who served in our American, British, and Italian forces, and even the Sudetenland resistance. They are a part of freedom's history, just like all who serve, and are a part of my history too.

My father was a commander in the US Navy, an elite pathologist in the Medical Corps. I was born in a naval hospital and raised on a tight, loving ship. Lining our hallways were our family's military medals and awards, in between citizenship certificates and photographs from generations past, all thanks to my genealogist mother. On my bedroom wall, surrounded by photographs of F-117s, F-22s, and B-2s, proudly hung a poem by John Gillespie Magee Jr.:

High Flight

Oh! I have slipped the surly bonds of Earth
And danced the skies on laughter-silvered wings;
Sunward I've climbed, and joined the tumbling mirth
of sun-split clouds—and done a hundred things
You have not dreamed of—wheeled and soared and swung
High in the sunlit silence. Hov'ring there,
I've chased the shouting wind along, and flung
My eager craft through footless halls of air . . .

Up, up the long, delirious, burning blue
I've topped the wind-swept heights with easy grace
Where never lark nor ever eagle flew—
And, while with silent lifting mind I've trod
The high untrespassed sanctity of space,
Put out my hand, and touched the face of God.

As I dreamed of one day slicing through the heavens in a fighter jet, I wondered—would I, too, be able to soar close to God?

I wasn't aware that, in December 1941, just four months after Magee began writing *High Flight*, he died after colliding his Spitfire VZ-H with a RAF training aircraft. At the young age of nineteen, Magee was already a combat veteran, having been the lone survivor of a Luftwaffe dogfight with leading German ace Joachim Müncheberg. His gallant service ended that same year, before he saw twenty, and more than three years before the world saw V-E Day. He lies buried in a small village in England, his coffin laid to rest by other pilots in his squadron, the verses of *High Flight* adorned on his tombstone.

Less than five hundred miles away in Suresnes, France, lies another young soldier in his final resting place, a casualty of the prior World War amid similar global grief. Private First Class Joseph Lorenz was a member of the US Army's American Expeditionary Force, Rainbow Division, who made the Ultimate Sacrifice at the age of twenty-one after sacrificing one of his legs earlier in the war. His tombstone has no verse on it, no poetry; only his name, rank, and battalion details, and the date of his death: NOV. 21, 1918.

But the memory of his mother's hand remains on the top of the tombstone after she visited his grave alongside three hundred and fifty other Gold Star mothers in 1930; his sister's, when she visited twice during her deployment with the US Army Nurse Corps during World War II; and years later, his great-niece's—my mother.

So it seemed a natural fit that the allure of service and duty beckoned me, too, from the glory of the sky. The long story "short" is that I was too small to be a fighter pilot, which required a minimum height of five feet, four inches. Thus I "peaked" at my Cadet of the Quarter Award while in the US Air Force Reserve Officers' Training Corps (ROTC) at the University of Washington.

But a different accolade was just as impactful to me at that young age, which came in the form of a simple anecdote by the detachment commander, a colonel. He told me he had gone to the renowned Tulip Festival in the Skagit Valley and noticed in a field of all-red tulips, there was one single yellow tulip growing proudly. "Cadet Compagno, you remind me of that yellow tulip," he declared. I brimmed with pride. In an environment where being or looking different was discouraged, I knew what he meant.

He meant Christ's light was visibly shining through me. What else could it be?

The psalmist tells us the Lord is our refuge and our fortress, our God in Whom we trust, under Whose wings we will be protected, His faithfulness our shield and rampart. For our warfighters, there is no greater test than the brutal demands of war. Violent battles and long deployments test resolve and courage; the anguish of loss due to the Ultimate Sacrifice and family separation distresses even the strongest hearts. Every role soldiers play in the constellation of combat requires above-and-beyond perseverance, determination, and bravery. Sometimes miracles are required. But with God, all things are possible. The stories you are about to read reveal just that.

PART I

The Global
War on Terror

Me (*far right*) with my fellow Raiderettes on
our USO tour in front of the best mode of travel ever:
the Black Hawk.

Me (*center*) during our Sadr City slumber
party in Iraq, 2009.

Colonel Tim Karcher supporting his troops while on
patrol in Sadr City, Iraq, 2009.

Family for a Night and Always

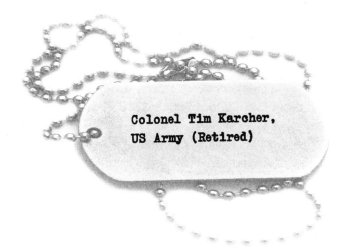

Colonel Tim Karcher,
US Army (Retired)

In June 2009, while an NFL cheerleader for the then–Oakland Raiders, I had the honor of visiting the US troops deployed to Kuwait and Iraq alongside four of my fellow Raiderettes. It was an incredible two weeks and the privilege of a lifetime to serve as an ambassador from home for those brave men and women serving our country so far away. We visited numerous forward operating bases (FOB) in addition to the main Baghdad bases, with Black Hawk helicopters flying us everywhere we went. (Every year since, I ask Santa for one. Best mode of transport ever.) We spent hours with the troops, just talking and getting to know them, in addition to holding nightly performances and structured meet-and-greets, with a gamut of additional activities, from a pool party with Special Forces in one of Saddam Hussein's palaces (can't make it up) to "dance-offs" with the soldiers (their idea) to sobering history tours led by ally Iraqis. It was important to us that we boost morale and let those men and women know how deeply their country supported and valued them.

Before we made the trip, I was interviewed on local radio stations throughout the San Francisco Bay Area and asked members of the community to write letters to the troops that I could bring to them. Hundreds of letters poured in. One of my favorite parts of the nightly shows was when the five of us would sit on the edge of the stage and I would read some of them aloud. One memorable letter was from the father of one of my dear friends. He had served in Vietnam and his letter was so poignant that tears flowed, ours and theirs. So many people had sent in cards and letters we were able to leave many at every FOB and main base we visited, and it moved me deeply to see soldiers reading those special notes from home.

The whole experience was inspiring and enlightening. At the larger bases we shopped in the post exchange (PX); I'm pretty sure our cutting Army T-shirts into cute tank tops and tie-ups wasn't regulation-approved! We were surprised that change was given in paper tokens instead of coins; I kept a "quarter" that had a photo of a soldier with an Iraqi child in my wallet after that as a reminder of the men and women serving and sacrificing so far from home. Visits with the wounded and the medical staff in field clinics and the main hospital in Baghdad were poignant highlights I will always carry in my heart. It was significant watching the soldiers return from foot patrols through the congested streets, laden with gear and weapons, dusty, sweaty, having just undergone such a dangerous mission. My heart went out to them and I prayed for their continued safety and protection. My hope was that we provided a welcome (safe) distraction, an uplifting bright spot in the day for those brave, young soldiers.

Of course, you can't bring cheerleaders anywhere without them stunting . . . even in war. At one of the FOBs, we encountered a soldier who had been a cheerleader. Everyone was thrilled to have a base, and he was thrilled to have flyers! I'll never forget seeing my fellow Raiderette balancing on one foot on a single upstretched arm of the soldier dressed in his camouflage fatigues (a stunt known, aptly, as the "Liberty"), with the wide desert and Army equipment all around us. I think our team director had a belated heart attack when she learned we had been stunting without safeties!

At another one of our stops, a young soldier brought his guitar to our meet-and-greet. He began strumming and singing Jason Mraz's "I'm Yours." This sweet, acoustic version was so charming and heartfelt. Our Black Hawk touched down and we all had to run out, with tears in our eyes, to the lovely, fading strains of that troubadour still playing his heart out for us. Many soldiers even took patches off their uniforms and handed them to us, and these remain framed and cherished to this day. We created countless special memories over such a short period of time, and I will never forget the warmth and hospitality shown to us by these soldiers serving bravely during wartime.

There were also risks to our safety. Included on our itinerary was visiting the US Army FOB at Baghdad's Sadr City—one of the most dangerous FOBs. As such, it was a complete shock to anyone who saw our agenda that we were headed there—including the men actually stationed at the Sadr City FOB, who thought there must have been a mistake and there was no way we were coming. But indeed we arrived, excited and openhearted. It was a new experience for us to land in the median of what appeared to be a massive highway. Then we watched in surprise as an entire team of soldiers ran out of huge gates, stopped all traffic, and secured a perimeter with their M4s pulled. Then they beckoned to us, and we ran across the highway (yes, in our NFL uniforms—I can't imagine what the drivers in those cars were thinking) and into the gates to safety. The ultimate game of Red Rover!

After we had been there a few hours spending time with the soldiers, we got the news that the Black Hawk that was scheduled to pick us up had been diverted for a medevac. No return time was scheduled; we were told only that it would come back when it could. So we ended up having to spend most of the night in that concrete, urban complex. No one went to bed; we all stayed up together, talking and playing games in the inner courtyard, laughing well into the night. It was like a summer camp, a special bonding experience, where the soldiers perhaps momentarily forgot the dangers surrounding us and only felt our shared joy of making new, lifelong friends. It was definitely my favorite night on the trip—likely one of my favorites ever. For those of us in that Sadr City slumber party, we were family.

I will never forget the commanding officer, then–Lieutenant Colonel Tim Karcher, telling us firmly that he had three daughters at home so he wasn't going to sleep until we were safely and soundly out of there. While we were happy at the news of the extended stay, I'm pretty sure his blood pressure hit the roof over the added security risks of his bright and smiley houseguests. On the outside, at least, his demeanor was unflappable—the utmost gentleman of a host. We knew we were in the best hands.

In the wee hours of the morning, the Black Hawk returned. The party ended and we had to run out, with barely a proper goodbye and thank you to those special soldiers in Sadr City.

Three days later, those men drove over an improvised explosive device (IED). Lieutenant Colonel Karcher lost his legs (and his life, many times, each time being resuscitated against all odds). After his medevac, the team drove over another IED. Sergeant Timothy David lost his life. It was twenty-eight-year-old Sergeant David's fourth tour of duty in Iraq, and sixth tour of duty total. He was younger than I was.

Fifteen years later, Colonel Karcher and I reunited. This is our story.

Unlikely Houseguests

One of nine administrative districts in Baghdad, Sadr City is among the poorest. A single public housing project has over one million residents. The year before we visited, in 2008, Iraqi insurgents had intensified their attacks against US forces and the Iraqi troops they were there to support. By the time we arrived, a cease-fire had been in place for a number of months. But earlier that month, a bombing at a market killed at least 69 civilians and injured more than 150 others. That was the nature of this war. Volatility remained.

Against that backdrop, Colonel Karcher was told five NFL cheerleaders were going to visit. And then he learned we were stranded there! He described what went through his mind: "This was one of those 'Thou shalt not fail' missions!" he said, laughing.

"When you get visitors, you have to roll out the red carpet. Let me put this in a different context: You can imagine having unexpected houseguests you want to impress. Only they're coming just after a tornado has come through and the sewage lines are busted, and you have no nice place to house your guests. And you have to understand this. We lived in *trailers*, Emily. We jokingly called ourselves 'trailer trash.' Those trailers had been used and abused. We had two 'VIP' trailers; the only thing VIP about them was that they had sheets that might have been cleaned that week. So as soon as we got word that your aircraft got diverted, well, soon after the tapestry of profanity escaped my lips, I told my operations officer in no uncertain terms he needed to find me another aircraft!"

After we stopped laughing, he proceeded. "Next, Plan B was to get somebody over to those VIP trailers, scrub them down, find sheets that aren't gross, and, if we could have found any (and there weren't any), put flowers in the room." We bantered about what I feared had been an unexpected burden, which the colonel assured me was actually a gift. "To be honest though," Tim told me, "I think that if your helicopter hadn't been diverted, some of the guys would have fired warning shots at it to drive it off so that you could have stayed longer. We were a small joint security station in the armpit of nowhere. We literally had three acres of property surrounded by a wall and guard towers and an entry control point. We didn't even have a helicopter landing zone. You came in and landed in the middle of a four-lane divided highway and we had to hustle all of you inside."

Man, I knew Sadr City was rough, but I had no idea those poor guys had been scrambling behind the scenes to fashion a Ritz-Carlton out of dust. We would have been happy sleeping outside all night—but the gentlemen in these soldiers shone through.

And the thought that our stay instigated panic—I was still half-laughing at the colonel's description and half-mortified we had caused these warriors likely more stress than the insurgents did.

The Scent of Courage

Of course, Tim wasn't complaining about the conditions. He was making a point about how amazed and pleased they were that the USO sent us to their location. He and everyone under his command were thrilled because the smaller—and more dangerous—outposts like his didn't get visitors very often. Instead, dignitaries and celebrities went to the larger bases. So when he got word that the NFL was coming to their little corner of the war, they appreciated it and wanted to crank up the hospitality. Tim also wanted to be sure that as many of the 1,000-plus troops under his command spread out across four total outposts could attend as possible. It was deeply humbling to learn how much coordination, communication, and resources went into (what should have been) our relatively brief visit.

Also a lot of personal preparation, apparently. After we were ushered inside, Tim had collapsed the security perimeter and was walking along when he ran into one of his younger staff sergeants. "I smelled him before I saw him," Tim gleefully recalled. He didn't want to mention the staff sergeant's name, to avoid embarrassing him, but Tim said he was a "good-looking young man." Tim noticed that he had on a perfectly fresh uniform, when earlier he'd been covered in dust, and the young lad was clean-shaven to boot. The only thing not fresh about him was the sweat dripping off him in that June heat. Then Tim caught a whiff of something unfamiliar in that environment. Horrified, he began sniffing—wrinkling his nose, he sputtered, "Dude, you aren't wearing *aftershave*, are you?"

Tim was aghast and thought it was hilarious. "He rolled his eyes and shook his head, pleading with me, 'Please, sir, don't give me crap,'" Tim remembered. But he couldn't resist: "'Where did you find aftershave in Iraq? Do you mean to tell me you brought that with you? And what is your intention here? These women are only going to be here for two hours!' I could see him cringing at the fact that I was teasing him—and for good reason," Tim said. "Finally, I told him that if he thought that this encounter with the five of you cheerleaders was going to lead to anything, then he was a sad, sad, strange little man."

We cackled. Looking back, I'm crossing my fingers that one of us girls told the young chap that he indeed smelled lovely.

"But I should have suspected something like that was going to happen," Tim said. "After all, your visit was the main topic of conversation before you got there and everybody talked about it again for even more days after. Also, whether you guys knew it or not, there were two soldiers right outside the trailer you were staying in. We didn't need that level of security. But they were there to make sure nobody came around, trying to get a peek at the beautiful ladies."

We were having so much fun we didn't realize just how much effort had gone into protecting us from harm. On a broader scale, hearing these details emphasized what I had felt at the time. Our visits mattered a great deal. For them we were a slice of home, a breath of fresh air, a moment to slip outside the realities of war and just *be*. At a minimum, a night of entertainment to break up the monotony of battle—and the comforting knowledge that America was sending ambassadors representing the support, love, and prayers of millions back home.

"The fact that your trip was extended was an example of the good Lord blessing us," Tim shared. "I think that it made the whole thing more relaxed. They got to interact with you instead of you just coming in and hustling back out. They enjoyed the show you performed, but this was different, this was special. I thank the good Lord for giving us that day together. It really did raise spirits. So you accomplished your mission, and we accomplished ours."

This brave colonel, this leader to so many soldiers under his command who were all serving for our freedoms, calling *us* the blessing! My heart grew three sizes. I doubt any of them realize—although I pray they all know—they raised our spirits too.

The Best of Us

While there, I learned many varied reasons these soldiers had signed up for service. They shared about driving passions, financial hardship, family needs, and everything in between. Tim and I reflected on the kinds of young, brave men and women I had met there. "I spent twenty-six years in the military," Tim said, "and one of the great joys of that time was seeing how a cross sampling of our country serves. The military is a microcosm of our country. You can see how divided we are as a country, but you don't see that in the military. You don't experience that. People from all walks of life serve alongside one another."

He described the broader US military mission as well, which included a larger no-ble cause. These soldiers were doing very important work. "Our mission wasn't just to bring security, but to reestablish or instigate a quality of life for the people there. It was so much more than just a fight," Tim told me. "We were trying to bring them essen-tial services—electricity, flowing water, sanitation. Hard to believe those things weren't there in the capital city of the country. Some of the Iraqis saw us as occupiers, that we'd toppled their government, and so they fought us. And we engaged in fights each and every day, and each and every night. And even if it weren't for that, our soldiers were doing something heroic for those people."

At times in Iraq, and especially in Sadr City, I was overcome with a sense of deep pride for these troops. For their earnest, selfless commitment day after day to duty and to our country. It was my privilege to spend time with them, these bright stars of our country, joyful and funny and warm and all independently unique in the midst of the constant looming risk of injury or death. They serve with distinction, with honor, and with a loyalty that shines through when the worst occurs.

The Bright Light

We had no idea that the worst would occur for Tim and the soldiers of the Sadr City FOB just after we left. "June 28, 2009. Literally three or four days after your visit, we were closing down our base camps inside Sadr City," Tim began. "The one you visited us at was shut. We had moved to one just outside the city. And we were working on closing the others as a part of an agreement the US had made, a status force agreement, with the Iraqi government. We were going to leave one in place, and that's where I was operating from. Anytime we closed one, there would be a ceremony and some representative of the prime minister would be there. Generally, they were politicians. On this one occasion, I knew that I had to be the one on our side to attend. I tried to make all of them, but this one I knew I needed to be at. I'd received the schedule for the day and it included who the Iraqi guy was going to be. To put it politely, he was a bit of a jerk. I knew that I didn't want to put one my subordinates in a bad place and have to deal with him. They don't get paid enough for that.

"And, as fate would have it, this was one of those really windy Iraqi days. All aircraft were grounded so we were going to have to drive to this one, this last of the closures. This would take up a big chunk of the day, but there were about one hundred of our soldiers there. And I felt a duty to be there for them. We were driving along, and it was basically a brownout; we could see maybe fifty feet in front of us. We arrived in this crowded, tightly packed town. We got to an intersection and had to slow way down to make the turn.

"I heard a big boom. I know immediately what's going on. You hear it, you feel it, you see it, taste it. So, I yelled over my shoulder since I knew all our comms were taken out. The vehicle is full of dust and smoke. I yelled to my guys, 'I've got two broken legs. How's everybody else?' They all report back that they're okay.

"I took a little more time, knowing that everybody else was good, to assess my situation more thoroughly. The pain made me think my legs were broken. They weren't. They were *gone*. I looked at the rifle that I always carried with the stock on the floorboards and the barrel was pointing up. It was busted in half. So, I yelled to the guys, 'Correction on that last report. My rifle's in two pieces. I got no legs. I'm no use to you guys anymore.'

"I thought I passed out at that point, but later on my guys were able to fill me in. I had remained conscious. So, my next question to them was, 'Okay, was I screaming like a six-year-old girl?' Thankfully, they told me I wasn't. I'd remained calm. That was huge for me because nobody wants to lose cool points."

Only Tim could make me laugh while sharing this deeply harrowing story. He shared that the guys later told him that he had been completely lucid, calmly discussing ways they could get him out of the vehicle. The door had been hit with four different devices and would not open. "They had to pick me up and hand me over the radio mount to get me out the driver's door. They lay me down on the ground next to the car where the insurgents had placed the bomb in the trunk. The medic was by my side placing tourniquets—and then the gas tank of that car burst. Just like in the movies, the medic sprawled over me, protecting me with his body. A lot of folks saved my life that day."

The colonel's men got him back to a battalion aid station, where a physician's assistant worked on him for about an hour. Because of the high winds and the dust storm, no aircraft could fly to medevac him out. So he was loaded into an armored ambulance. But before that, the unthinkable happened.

"I died," Tim reported. Amid my shock, he went on: "And later, I gave that physician's assistant a hard time about that. I told him, 'You let me die. You suck.' He wasn't putting up with that and said, 'No, sir. You're a quitter!' Obviously they got my heart started again. I wish I had a story about seeing a bright light and all that, but I don't."

Tim was then, and still is, a bright light himself. So was his sergeant major, his go-to guy who told them that even if Tim had no vital signs, they were putting him in that ambulance no matter what. After eight hours at a combat support hospital in Baghdad, the doctors finally stabilized him. After that it was on to Landstuhl, Germany, and the Landstuhl Regional Medical Center, a Level II Trauma Center and the largest American hospital outside the US.

There were many brothers who saved Tim's life, whose healing hands were laid on him, whose prayers covered him, and who ensured he was never alone. "I don't remember much of the week I spent there. A former commander of mine was stationed in Germany. I had been his second in command, and back in California, the two of us ran Bible studies out of our houses. He heard what had happened to me, and he went to his commander, a four-star general, who, it just so happened, knew me. So my friend, my brother in Christ, got permission to come to Landstuhl, and he stayed by my side the entire time I was there. When I was going to be shipped to the US to be treated at Walter Reed [National Military Medical Center in Washington, D.C.], he flew back on the medical evacuation helicopter with me. He got me to Walter Reed and then handed me off to my wife. His work was complete."

Laughing Through Tears

Tim's recovery was just beginning. Throughout it all, Tim's faith remained rock solid and his humor intact. He was provided with plenty of help over the next few months, although sometimes the help wasn't helpful. His former commander had arranged for a chaplain to visit him at Walter Reed. Out of nowhere, the chaplain told Tim it was okay for him to be "angry at God" about the loss of his legs, to which Tim retorted, "God promised me eternal life, not eternal legs!"

Tim's family provided unwavering, irreplaceable support during the arduous recovery process. His wife served as the central pillar of that support, remaining by his side from the moment she could and keeping friends and family updated on his condition. He spent six weeks at Walter Reed and had, as he put it, "a few ups and downs." One of those "down" times was when his heart stopped beating.

"I died there as well. I remember as it was happening that I was really, really sad. Not scared, because I knew where I was going. I was sad to leave my wife, my daughters behind. I was going to miss out on walking my daughters down the aisle, that kind of stuff. But I also knew this: hundreds and hundreds of people were praying for me. And it was a rough, rough time. I had all kinds of infections, a fever of 105."

Tim learned many of these details much later, when he read the CaringBridge entries his wife posted regularly. "At one point, she took my hand and told me it was okay if I needed to let go. She and the girls would be okay. My wife's faith is more astounding and deep than mine is, or anyone else's. My wife was a rock for our kids. She kept everyone motivated. She kept everybody informed. She never stopped praying. She never stopped believing.

"Later on, of course, I learned about her saying it was okay for me to let go." And in true Tim fashion, he joked that he was now going to stop paying his life insurance premiums because it had been "way too freaking easy for her to tell me it was okay if I let go!" Yet again, I was laughing through my tears.

True Bravery

In just one example of his wife's incredible strength, she successfully fought against all military regulations and procured a way for her and their daughters to see and hold Tim for the first time after his massive injuries, on the tarmac at Fort Hood. Tim was on a medical flight that had to stop over at Fort Hood in Texas before proceeding to San Antonio; his wife battled all the way up the chain of command to get permission for her and their daughters to come out on the tarmac and onto the aircraft. A photo captured that moment, now one of his favorites.

Years later he found out that his older daughter hated the photograph—it was a reminder of her abject fear in that moment. At the time, she was convinced that the reason they were visiting him on a tarmac was because it was the last time she would ever see him. She thought she was saying goodbye to her father. Tim has seen people do a lot of courageous things in his life; he told me that his daughter facing her fears to see him was at the top of his list of acts of bravery. For the rest of us, Tim's bravery tops that list too.

Greater Love

Tim spent two years in San Antonio learning to walk with prostheses. And then (to no one's surprise who has spent even one moment with this determined man of steel), he opted into the limited duty program the Army offered so he could return to work. But he made an important distinction: "It wasn't that I loved the Army. I loved the *soldiers*. I loved taking care of them, helping them and their families. Being a commander was an extraordinarily rewarding sacred duty."

Tim always felt an obligation to the men under his command and to his fellow soldiers. Notably, the IED attack that took his legs was not his first serious battle injury. He had been shot in the left arm prior to that. He was sent back home to recover and rehabilitate for five months. He was happy to be there (except for having to paint the interior of the house). He knew that it was highly unlikely he'd die from his wounds. But as time went on, something nagged at him. His unit was in Iraq and was taking more casualties than any other unit deployed there. He felt horribly guilty that his buddies were out there fighting and dying, while he was home safe. He prayed for them regularly.

"I learned during my time in combat that everybody's afraid of something. My biggest fear as a commander, as an officer, was ordering soldiers out into battle. Good commanders go out and share the danger, but you're rarely the guy who goes through the door first in a breaching maneuver. You're not doing the most dangerous jobs. And the thing that terrified me was I didn't know if these young soldiers were saved or not. Am I not only condemning them to death on earth, but for all eternity? The focus of my prayer life was asking the Lord to open the hearts of my soldiers to Him. So that if they did die, they didn't die for eternity. That felt like a huge burden, more so than if they were killed in action; to die for all eternity—*that* was a tough one to contemplate."

Heavy lies the burden of command. We spoke about Sergeant Timothy David and the loss of his priceless life after Tim was medevaced. "As a commander you can't just send your guys and say, 'Good luck, boys. I'll be out on the porch drinking coffee.' So, me and our sergeant major would go out every day, separately, to spend time with one of the units out there in the field. And we'd be accompanied by a security detail. And we had a running joke between the sergeant major and his detail, and me and mine. Whoever went out first would say, 'I've got route clearance for you.' What we meant was, we'd detonate whatever IEDs were along the road to make it safe for your later passage. Gallows humor, but that was how we joked around.

"Sergeant David was a member of our sergeant major's detail. On the day I got injured, Sergeant David and his unit came to the scene. I got loaded in the armored ambulance, and three other armored vehicles escorted that ambulance across town. It took about an hour to get me to that hospital. My sergeant major and I were—and are— good friends. He didn't want to leave the hospital until he knew I was somewhat stable. Eight hours of surgery later, I was. By that time night had fallen.

"At that point, my sergeant major needed to get back to the base to help support my second in command [to] take over. And that's when it started; that's when they were hit. We all know the Bible verse that says, 'Greater love hath no man, than to lay down his life for his friends (John 15:13).' Tim David died, so I could have life."

God Gave Me You

Tim and his wife were joined together by divine appointment, ironclad in their shared faith from the outset. "My wife is my best faith companion. She really brought me back to church shortly after we were newly married. I know that she's the one that God made for me. He put us together and I didn't really realize what I was getting. We went on our first date on October twenty-third of 1989 and I asked her to marry me on the eighth of December that year (not that I remember those kinds of things!). So, six weeks. I admit that I was graduating and getting ready to go off to the Army, but I just knew. And later I realized how little I knew. I didn't fully realize who it was that God had set me up with and who God had put me in this life with. I am so blessed to have her, someone to walk through this life with."

Tim's beautiful family continues to thrive, a joyful household built on rock. "I'm fortunate to have three daughters who I love dearly. My wife says that they keep me young. They also don't let me act like I'm anything special. Every year on the twenty-eighth of June, the anniversary of my IED day, my youngest daughter makes a cake and decorates it with one of those 'No' symbols—the word *legs* with a slashed circle around it. She gets that from me," he said, laughing proudly.

* * *

My fellow Raiderettes and I will likely never fully understand the protection and safety Colonel Karcher ensured us by staying by our side all those years ago in Iraq. What a blessing to have been reunited with this humble hero and his infectiously merry, indestructible spirit. I left Sadr City that night a better person, having served as a witness to selfless service and the sustained lengths our soldiers go to for our country and our freedoms. I left my reunion with Tim even better.

The depth of this man's elite leadership, heroic service and sacrifices, and buoyant spirit throughout it all blessed me then and blesses me now. Colonel Karcher is the kind of man who inspires you to be the best person you can be, the most noble in character, all the while keeping a laugh just under the surface, ready to spread delight. I knew God ordered our steps back to this connection and could imagine our Heavenly Father smiling just as big as I was. "Every good and perfect gift is from above" (James 1:17).

The power of prayer helped Colonel Karcher survive (over and over) and recover—among those prayers mine, as we had learned about those IEDs some months later via his wife. The power of his remarkable, unshakable faith colored his recovery in an unfaltering strength, a consistent security in knowing Jesus. This extraordinary story reveals the peace within that no tribulation can affect, not even multiple earthly deaths.

Men like Colonel Karcher are often reluctant to receive attention, their servant's hearts resisting the accolades they so richly deserve. When I reached out to him for this book, he explained he would make an exception. For Christ, and for me. "I would normally decline anything that focused attention on me, but I cannot in this case. The personal connection that we have requires that I help you in any way that I can. Additionally, I simply cannot pass up any opportunity to share how God has saved me (both physically and, more importantly, spiritually). I would be honored to help in any way that I can."

No, sir, the honor is all mine. Thank you for your extraordinary service—and for being family to us when we were so many miles from home.

If your spirit burns with light, fully illuminated with
no trace of darkness, you will be a shining lamp, reflecting rays
of truth by the way you live.

—LUKE 11:36

Me flying between forward operating
bases in Iraq in 2009.

Army Ranger Jeff Struecker posing
with his HMMWV

2

Thy Will Be Done

Chaplain, Major Jeff Struecker,
US Army, 75th Ranger Regiment
(Retired)

In 1993, then-Sergeant Jeff Struecker was the squad leader assigned to Task Force Ranger of the US Army's 75th Ranger Regiment. Twenty-four years old, Jeff had already seen major action in Operation Just Cause during the invasion of Panama in 1989, and then served in Kuwait during Operation Desert Storm. Already battle-tested, even he couldn't have anticipated what happened on his deployment to Somalia.

Jeff and the rest of Task Force Ranger were in Somalia to intervene in the Somali Civil War. A United Nations resolution called Operation Restore Hope had been passed to provide humanitarian aid. But members of a brutal terrorist organization, the Somali National Alliance, attacked and killed a number of United Nations peacekeeping troops, and also intercepted much-needed relief supplies for the drought-stricken people. The American military launched Operation Gothic Serpent in response, with the mission for Task Force Ranger to capture the leader of the Somali National Alliance. What ensued during that mission became the longest continuous firefight the US Army had engaged in since the Vietnam War. The harrowing story was later the subject of a bestselling book and an Academy Award–winning film, *Black Hawk Down*.

On October 3, Jeff's squad was tasked with rescuing Private First Class Todd Blackburn, who fell while attempting to fast-rope from a Black Hawk helicopter. Two Black Hawks were shot down by members of the Somali National Alliance. During the fifteen-hour raging battle, eighteen soldiers were killed, including two Delta Force operatives. Devastated Americans, and others around the world, were further horrified when footage emerged of a dead US soldier's body being dragged through the streets by terrorists. What had been a peacekeeping mission turned into the Battle of Mogadishu.

During the middle of this ferocious firefight, it suddenly became clear to Jeff—he was 100 percent convinced—that he was going to die. He was a seasoned combat veteran, had been shot at before, and knew exactly what he was getting into. And he knew with conviction that nobody would survive.

One of the first men killed was sitting just twelve inches away from Jeff when he took a mortal round in the head. Even at that initial point, everybody around Jeff believed—also with 100 percent certainty—that they were all going to die. "Way too many bad guys, way too many bullets," Jeff stated. Nobody was going to make it out of this one alive.

But Jeff did. And the part of the story you might not know—the part that might be the most miraculous of all—is what happened *after* he survived.

Saved

In his youth, Jeff asked a lot of hard questions. Specifically, he was wrestling with the afterlife: What is it like? Where do you go and who gets to go there? But Jeff's family was atheist. No one read the Bible. No one talked about God, and there was no prayer. And so no one in his family knew the answers. Jeff was about as lost as a human being can be, because not only did he not know Christ personally, but he didn't even know a single Christian.

"And then God saw fit, when we lived in an apartment complex, to send me these next-door neighbors across the hall," Jeff recalled. "I was thirteen years old. They shared the gospel with me. And that night, Jesus radically saved me. And the next morning, man, I was different—totally different. Because I was living in a family of atheists, I just got up as a teenager and started walking [to] the nearest church. Whatever denomination was okay with me. I had no church background to base my decision on."

Then Jeff joined the Army. He was still in high school and left his small town in Iowa on a whim. "I really was just looking for a way out of my hometown," Jeff told me. "I come from a farming community, and if you don't have a farm, you don't have a future. And I didn't have a farm. Once in, I fell in love with the Ranger Regiment. The dudes I had a chance to work with, the missions we went on. The Ranger Regiment shaped me into the man that I became, nearly more than anything, except for my relationship with Christ and with my wife."

Jeff served with the Rangers for most of his career, serving twenty-three years in the Army with sixteen Ranger Regiment combat deployments, nine of them in Afghanistan and five in Iraq. As Jeff developed and sharpened his iron Ranger skills, especially in those early years of service, so too did he sharpen the iron of his faith. "It wasn't until I joined the Army and ironically spent ten years in one duty station that I really got plugged into a church. I really got discipled and my faith really grew deep."

Jeff wore his faith on his sleeve, and everybody in the unit knew what he believed in. He didn't force his faith on anyone, didn't introduce the topic in conversation. But when faith did come up, Jeff was bold about it. "And as a result, over time, I kind of developed this reputation so that others would say, 'Hey, watch your language around Jeff. He doesn't drink. He doesn't use the kind of language like everybody else. Jeff is one of those guys you gotta [mind] your P's and Q's around.'"

Jeff led by example and didn't admonish other Rangers for language or behavior—with one exception. "Well, I did call them out when they used the Lord's name in vain. Maybe that was it. But the rest of it, I was just like, hey, whatever, man, you do you."

Jeff continued to share his faith boldly. He was leading Bible studies in the barracks, talking to guys about his faith. And most of them were incredibly tough, very talented, and exceptionally smart and fit guys, who had conquered the world through their own abilities.

"They are that good," Jeff recalled. "And so, when I tried to talk to them about Jesus, their basic answer was, 'Hey, you can have that Jesus stuff, Jeff. It's a crutch. And I don't need it because I'm good enough that I don't need Jesus or whatever you believe in.' And that was the kind of standard answer I got for the first few years in the Army."

And that remained the case until October 3, 1993, when he and the rest of his squad were faced with their seemingly inevitable deaths. For all their fortitude, for all their talent, for all their intelligence and elite capabilities, they couldn't conquer the harsh reality they faced when they went into the teeth of the battle in Mogadishu—not once, not twice, but three times over the course of that day and night.

Trial by Fire

"We were thrown into Somalia," Jeff told me. "I'd never done missions on vehicles before. I didn't even know how to drive those military vehicles. We got a few days to train before we jumped on transport aircraft to Somalia. One of my guys, Brad Paulsen, a gunner, got a few sessions on the range firing a .50-cal machine gun, and that was it."

The mission escalated immediately, with a threat that one could have expected. "A few days before those Black Hawks went down, we got into a firefight where we were taking rounds from three different directions. At first, I thought the first rounds I heard were a kid setting off firecrackers. And then a couple of rounds slipped by me; an RPG went right by me and went off right behind us. There were bad guys firing from a reviewing stand in the streets. We took care of that pretty quick.

"But that was the first time we were under accurate enemy fire. And it turned out, it wasn't the bad guys who were getting close to us; it was friendly fire. The Tenth Mountain Division was firing at us accidentally. That is not uncommon. You have different units out there and they are not aware of what the other is doing or where they're positioned. They heard and saw shots, so they returned fire on the same guys we were after.

"By God's grace, no American killed another American. But it was pretty chaotic with fire coming at us from all around, the Somalis firing from a hospital—in defiance of the Geneva Convention—and little birds [helicopters] flying all around. If nothing else, we got some live-action training in fighting from vehicles, and Brad got really good with the .50-cal."

A few days later, that first firefight would feel like a mere training exercise. Even before PFC Todd Blackburn fell and lay wounded, Jeff and his squad were out in the tightly packed and narrow streets of Mogadishu, maneuvering into position under the command of Army Colonel Danny McKnight. Then a wrong turn—a typically innocuous error—put all their lives at risk.

"We rolled out in the city streets to get to the target building. Our squad was in two vehicles, mine and Danny Mitchell's behind us. We turned a half a block too early. That was scary. I'm looking around, and thought, *Hold on, wait a second. I can't cover us. I can't keep us safe here.* There were people, Somali civilians, everywhere. We became the easiest target. I said to Danny, 'We made a mistake. We need to get out of here. We need to get out of here really fast.' Finally, we get to our little holding position, waiting for the call to come pick up the assault force."

But another call came instead. "That's when we got the call to extract Blackburn," Jeff said. "We had to fight our way to his location. One of our guys is down, and who knew what kind of shape he was in, but we had to get to him. We had to fight our way there, and I noticed we were taking intense fire from a dude in a tree. We pulled up to an intersection. And I got a better view of the guy who's nearly completely hidden in this tree. He's firing effectively at us and near Blackburn. I told Brad to take out that tree with his .50-cal—it would go right through that tree. Brad fired two or three rounds and that target, that sniper rifle, went silent. No more problems from that tree, let's put it that way."

Thanks in large part to Brad's efficacy with the .50-cal, the men made it to Blackburn and loaded him into their vehicle. "We had one Humvee in front of him (the one I was riding in), the one carrying him, and then a third behind him. We were going to get him to the surgeon, drop him off, and then the plan was for us to turn right back around and help exfil [extract]the assault force back to the airfield."

God Speaks

Jeff began to describe how the battle sharply turned from horrible to horrifying. "When we drove down that narrow alleyway and turned on to a big sand road—what happened on that road, I've never seen anything, never experienced anything like it before. I've never experienced anything like it since then. We started getting hit from every single building, every window, every doorway, everywhere on both sides, ahead of us, behind us.

"There was a guy hiding under the bushes on the right. He was right next to our Humvee, and he had his AK-47 pointed right at Brad's back. Dominick Pilla, who was in our vehicle right next to me, fired a round and took that guy out.

"Almost simultaneously, Pilla took a round to the forehead and died instantly. Over the sound of the gun battle, I heard someone shouting *Pilla is dead! Pilla is dead!* We still had to get Blackburn back inside the wire. It was like parting the Red Sea. So many people were in the road, and we were taking fire."

Defying all odds of the staggering firefight, the men finally got back and offloaded PFC Blackburn. He would survive his wounds. Sergeant Dominick Pilla did not.

Four years prior, after the intense Battle of Rio Hato Airfield in 1989, Jeff had been responsible for taking all the wounded Rangers to the surgeon, and moving all the dead Rangers in filled body bags back to the casualty collection point. He knew how emotionally crushing and physically punishing cleaning up the remains of fellow Rangers was.

Right when the men returned to base and got off the Humvees, they were notified that two Black Hawks were down—they needed to go back out there. But then one of the special operators in Jeff's squad pulled him aside and said, "Hey, Jeff, you need to go clean up your Humvee."

Sergeant Pilla had taken a mortal head wound inside the Humvee, and his remains had saturated the vehicle. Without running water, instead just a pallet-mounted water tank, some buckets, and a mop, Jeff knew how difficult the cleanup would be—both physically and emotionally. He said to the guys, "You don't have to do this. I won't make you do this. But I can use some help."

"The most terrifying moment of my life, hands down, was standing at the back of that Humvee cleaning up Dominick's body. His brain, bone, all of it splattered everywhere on the back of that truck," Jeff said. "I also remember the radio was still on, and I was listening to the fight. It was going really, really bad. And I remember saying, 'Just turn the radio off. I don't want to hear it right now.' It was so bad.

"But I also remember watching Brad, a guy who had never been around that kind of blood and bodies before. I can't believe what I'm seeing. This guy, he's been in the Army for maybe a year, year and a half—been in the Ranger Regiment for just a little while. Never, ever been in a circumstance like this. And he's doing one of the most gruesome things a warrior will ever have to do in combat. And he's holding it all together, where most people who have been around for twenty or thirty years couldn't hold it together."

With that unfathomable job done, Jeff and his men went back into the fight, hoping to get to the crash sites where two Black Hawk helicopters had been taken down by enemy rocket-propelled grenades.

After joining a large convoy of other vehicles, Jeff witnessed another series of Brad's actions that astounded him. Once again taking heavy fire, once again threading their way through the narrow seam of streets in crowded Mogadishu, Brad distinguished himself yet again.

Already suffering from a shrapnel wound to the forehead and with blood running down his face, Brad continued directing fire with his .50-cal. A rooftop sniper had been wreaking havoc from above. Brad and Jeff realized that the one option left to them to hit this concealed target was to use a hand grenade in very, very close quarters.

Adding to the extreme circumstances, Brad had sustained another shrapnel wound, this one to his right hand. Jeff had bandaged it, but it was clear to him that Brad was in enormous pain. Jeff even suggested that Brad take a seat in the back of the Humvee. He feared his gunner wouldn't be able to effectively fire the weapon. Brad refused. Several times that night Jeff urged Brad to step back. Each time Brad refused. It was *his* gun to man, *his* job to maintain, and he wasn't going anywhere.

Jeff marvels to this day at Brad's sheer will to continue, his mental toughness overriding the physical near-impossibility of his one-handed operation of the .50-cal, exhibiting extreme bravery in the face of such adverse challenges. Still in extreme pain and with the effective use of only one hand, Brad was at his position when the sniper problem arose.

Jeff said to him, "Brad, listen, man, that building is so close to us. If you throw that grenade, and it doesn't go off right away, all he has to do is pick it up and drop it over the side. And it's gonna land right on top of us. So I need you to cook this thing off." The average grenade has about a four- to five-second fuse, after you pop the spoon. Four to five seconds later that grenade is going to blow up.

"Brad, here's what I'm going to do," Jeff told him. "I'm going to count after you pop the spoon. And when I tell you to throw—*and don't you dare throw one second early*—you throw that thing." A few seconds later, he popped the spoon. "I counted, 'One thousand, two thousand, THROW!' I watched the grenade like it was in slow motion. And as soon as the grenade crossed the lip of the roof—BOOM—it blows up!" There were no more problems from the rooftop for the rest of the night.

Jeff shone with pride. "Brad did this with flaming-hot shrapnel in his right hand, and he put the grenade perfectly where it's supposed to be. This was his second firefight and he performed like that. Amazing."

Jeff and his squad went back out a third, excruciating time. The hours passed while these warriors sustained this historically interminable battle, undergoing incomprehensible violence and facing severely disadvantaged odds. When they finally made it back to the UN base, located in the Mogadishu soccer stadium, it hit Jeff just how vicious the battle had been and how enormous the losses were.

"It wasn't just our squad. The whole force had been shot up. I saw all these body bags laying in a row. I saw all of the medics trying to keep the wounded alive. PFC John "Doc" Stanfield was treating people; guys on litters, multiple guys who are clinging to life all around him, and he was trying to treat them one at a time."

After leading the last of the Humvees through the streets, Jeff was the last one to make it back to base. Exhausted and with the firefight finally over, at nine o'clock the next morning Jeff rolled in to the base. His buddies were waiting for him. As Jeff got out of the Humvee, "they grabbed me, they hugged me, they didn't want to let me go," he shared.

"I remember looking at our squad and wondering how anybody was still alive. How on earth did any one of us survive that? It had been nothing but blood and gore. To this day, I've always said it is solely because of God's grace that any of us are still alive. I should have been in Arlington National Cemetery. Not some of these other guys."

The whole remaining task force was standing under a hangar on the airfield. Jeff navigated a whole host of emotions as he looked at each of his squad members, the battle still fresh and the losses just beginning to sink in.

And then, God spoke to him.

"What I sensed was clearer than anything I've ever experienced in my life. It was not a burning bush—I never heard an audible voice—but I felt the Lord saying, *Jeff, you were able to fight the way you did last night, because you have already settled your death and eternity. And the rest of your buddies haven't. And they need somebody who understands them, knows what they're going through, who can look them in the eyes and talk to them. And I want you to be that guy.*"

I Want What You Have

That miraculous moment shaped the rest of Jeff's life. God had called him to the ministry. He felt it as clearly as if there had been an audible command.

But then something else emerged. His squad members all began to share that they noticed the incredible peace, the unwavering faith, that Jeff had carried with him throughout the battle. "Most of them were saying things like, 'Jeff, I heard something in your voice over the radio last night.' 'Jeff, I watched you in the city streets and we have the same training, we've been through the same experiences. But I'm telling you, you have something that I don't have. And whatever that is, I want that. And I want it right now.'

"So many of my buddies were immediately confronted with their mortality. They were telling me 'Jeff, I shouldn't be alive right now. I'm not sure if I get on a helicopter or a Humvee that I'm going to make it home to my family. *And I don't know where I'm going to spend eternity.* And you obviously do. I want what you have.'" These men were literally saying *I need you to tell me about Jesus right now.*

"And I sensed, and I saw, and I heard during that battle, paratroopers and Rangers around me who were freaking out because of the violence and certainty of death. And I could conduct myself on the battlefield, not worried about my mortality, not worried about my eternity, because it's settled. But I could also look at those guys questioning me in the eyes and say, 'Look, guys, I know exactly where I'm going to spend eternity. And I know exactly what you're going through.'

"'And I'm here to tell you, life is different when you're staring down the barrel of an enemy rifle, and Jesus Christ is the center of your world. There's some things you just don't have to worry about. So, I'm here to tell you, man, it's different when you have a rock-solid faith, than if you go out there and you don't know what happens to you after you take your last breath.'"

Thus began the first phase of Jeff's calling to minister, to share the knowledge of Christ and God's promise of eternal salvation with men and women who shared the rare, defining experiences of combat. "And, man, God gave me some amazing opportunities to do incredible ministry," Jeff said. "I can't take credit for any of it. He put me in the right places at the right time, and people were willing to listen."

The Peace That Surpasses All Understanding

But there is more to this story. Jeff had been specifically prepared for that moment on the tarmac, that life-changing calling from God. It had happened a few hours earlier, in the thick of the firefight—there had been a profound moment where the entire battle changed for Jeff, in the most fundamental way.

Throughout his time in Somalia, Jeff had been studying his morning devotionals, spending time reading the Bible every morning before the rest of the guys awoke. A few weeks before the battle, he had been reading the story of the night before the crucifixion, which Jesus spent in the Garden of Gethsemane. Jesus spent that evening in prayer, overcome by sorrow at his impending death and even sweating blood amid his crushed spirit. He asked the Holy Father to remove his cup of suffering. But then Jesus said, "*Not my will, but Yours be done*"(Luke 22:42). In Christianity, this signifies the moment of complete surrender by Jesus to His Heavenly Father, the complete acceptance of the sacrifice of God's only son—by whose stripes we are all healed—because God loves man so much.

"Part of my story is that God gave me the peace that surpasses all understanding earlier that day in the firefight," Jeff explained. And then he described exactly how that came about: "There was a moment when I was absolutely terrified and I was certain I was going to die.

"At that moment, I prayed. And while I was in that dark, bad place out there in the streets, coming in and going back out again, my mind went back several times to the prayer that Jesus prayed in the garden. 'God, I don't want to do this' is basically what Jesus was saying. And that's how I felt as I was getting ready to go back out there again.

Then I started reflecting on what else Jesus said to his Father: "'Yet not my will, but Yours be done.'"

Jeff repeated those words: *Not my will, but Yours be done.* And peace flooded in.

"At that moment, and after, I felt no fear whatsoever. Life was reduced to a simple proposition. Only one of two things could happen next: Maybe God does perform a miracle and I survive, go home to my wife, my high school sweetheart who's pregnant. Or maybe I catch one in the chest today. If I go home to Georgia, I'm a winner. If I take one in the chest, I go home to my Father in Heaven, and I'm a winner.

"No matter what happens next, I have nothing to worry about. So why freak out over what happens next? I'm going to be okay. Either God lets me live, or He takes me Home to be with Him. *I'm ready either way.* And that sense of things was like someone had thrown a switch and night turned into day. At least it did for me."

And the peace of God, which surpasses all understanding, will guard
your hearts and your minds in Christ Jesus.

—PHILIPPIANS 4:7

This peace is so utterly transformative because the source is He who spoke the world into existence, the Alpha and the Omega. It is not an earthly calm that comes from external surroundings; it is written in scripture as surpassing all understanding because the transformative nature—the all-consuming, otherworldly peace—defies all earthly explanation.

During the firefight, Jeff was listening to the voices over the radio, coming from throughout their forces, up and down the chain of command. The situation was going from bad to worse. And when they thought it couldn't get any worse, it got even worse still. And Jeff knew the operators were panicking. "I can hear it in their voices," he remembered. "I know every voice on that radio. Those guys are closer than my own family. And I know what makes them tick. And I can tell they're freaking out. But when I'm on the radio, I'm totally calm."

That is what Jeff's squad had noticed—it was impossible not to have noticed the intrinsic calm Jeff held. They, too, heard all the voices filled with panic. And they heard his peace.

It was a physical manifestation too. While moving from position to position on the streets of Mogadishu, everybody else was running with their head down, but Jeff was seemingly unaffected by the rockets landing to his right and bullets going inches over his head. "In fact, one or two times," he said, "I had to tell some of them, 'Look, those bullets are far enough over your head that they're not that big of a deal. And if you duck when you hear a bullet, it's already too late because the bullet has passed by you. Either you get hit or you don't get hit.'" He wasn't walking foolishly through the city streets; he was still tactically aware of what was happening around him. But he remained calm.

Believe On Jesus

After the fight, the operators had questions for Jeff. "They had questions about what happened to my buddy after he just took one in the chest and died," he recalled. "They asked what was going to happen to them after they died. Some asked really hard questions that I don't have an answer for—not then and not now. One of which is: *Why did God let this happen to us?*"

Jeff didn't pretend to have an answer to those questions—"They're above my pay grade!" But his deeply developed and enriched faith, and the preparation God ensured he had, meant that he knew how to answer—because he knew Who *did* have those answers. He knew that no matter the problem or the question, God was bigger than it all. "I don't try to answer the questions that only God can answer. But I do think God's big enough that He can handle questions like that, even if you grit your teeth and clench your fist when you're asking."

Timing was just as crucial as perspective. "The Black Hawk Down battle got everybody's attention because about half of the unit was either killed or wounded," Jeff said, "And everybody started realizing that if we go back out there, all of us are going to be killed or wounded. So, figure some things out about what happens to you after you die."

Jeff has often told his fellow warriors there is really no wrong time to ask those questions. "But the worst time to do it," he told me, "is when you're in the middle of a firefight. You probably want to have this one figured out before the bullets start flying, not in the middle of a fight."

Jeff offered his guys a few more things to consider. "Those guys needed to know what to do *right now*. And I told them they needed to believe on Jesus. They thought I misspoke. 'You mean we need to believe *in* Jesus.' No. No. Believe *on* Jesus. This is where I believe our language is inaccurate. The idea of 'believe in Jesus' has become too much like 'believe in this historical figure from a long time ago.' Jesus has become like someone you read about in a book, no different from George Washington or Abraham Lincoln. No, actually what God is doing, what God asks of us, is to believe *on* Him."

Jeff was in airborne units almost his entire career. He uses this parachute analogy to explain better what he means about "in" versus "on": "You get on an airplane, you strap a parachute on your back. The plane flies around with the doors open, the green light goes on, and you can swear to me until you're blue in the face that you believe *in* this parachute. But you haven't really believed *on* the parachute, you really haven't exercised your faith, until you actually step out of the door of the airplane and see if that parachute is going to open."

After the fight, Jeff told his buddies that God asks us to take that first step, and then He will meet us after that. "But faith in Jesus is taking a step into the darkness and saying, *If this parachute doesn't open, then I'm going to burn in on this drop.*" A total and utter freefall of a surrender. "That's what the Bible means by faith. That's what the word *believe* means."

Divine Appointments

The incredible success of Jeff's tarmac ministry, the power of the Lord speaking to Jeff in that moment and crystallizing his purpose then and for the rest of his days, lies in this miraculous statistic: every one of those men became a Christian.

"Since Somalia, I don't know one of them today who hasn't become a Christian," Jeff told me. "Almost one hundred percent of the guys that were there in the fight with me said that they shouldn't be alive today. There must be a God in heaven. He must have given me a second chance, and He must have given me a second chance for a reason. I've personally had a chance to share Jesus with more than a few of them. Almost all of them follow this thought pattern: God gave me a second chance. I don't know why He did, but there must be a real God out there, and I'm going to give my life to Him in some form or fashion."

The day after the Battle of Mogadishu in Somalia changed the rest of Jeff's life. "God threw me a curveball," Jeff said. "As clear as anything I've ever felt in my life. And I didn't want it, wasn't looking for it, and never expected it in a million years. I just loved being a Ranger sergeant. I loved kicking in doors and killing bad guys, and I thought I was going to do that for the rest of my life—until God called me into the ministry."

There were two very definitive points in Jeff's career when he felt God had wired him together and put him on planet Earth for exactly that moment.

One of those moments was when he was a sergeant in the Ranger Regiment. It was a moment of euphoria that hit him, a surety of purpose. "I love Jesus, I love being a Ranger, I love doing what I do for my country," Jeff described feeling. "This is it, God put me on [this] planet Earth to do this. And I'm gonna keep doing this until God takes me home or until God tells me to do something different." That sheer joy and driving purpose is partly why Jeff was so effective in the Ranger Regiment. It inspired him to compete and win the Best Ranger Competition; it was because he truly loved it all. "And it's deep," Jeff said. "I've got a love deep in my bones all the way to tomorrow."

The second time was when Jeff was serving as chaplain to 2nd Ranger Battalion. "The war in Iraq and Afghanistan was just kicking off and starting to spin up, with lots of blood, lots of violence." One morning, the Rangers had just come back home after a combat deployment. They had lost some of their men on that deployment. Yet they were getting turned around and ready to go right back into the fight just weeks later. And as Jeff walked from his office to one of their company headquarters across a grass field, he knew again, "This is it." His certain purpose.

God had put him through all those experiences as a sergeant in the Ranger Regiment so that he could be the exact chaplain that those Rangers needed in that moment. And he wasn't going to take it lightly. He wasn't going to take it for granted.

Jeff vowed, "God, only You could wire my past in such a way that this unit needs a chaplain with immense combat experience. And I just happened to be a guide with that kind of experience. And all of the theological education and the experience working in ministry, at the same time—only You could put all of these together at a moment in the global war on terrorism when these guys needed it the most."

Our passions and purpose are placed on our heart because we are appropriately equipped and anointed to pursue and achieve them. When varying threads pull together and suddenly a tapestry in our life is revealed, we know it's God behind the synthesis. It's our steps being ordered, it's us being known and approved before we were even born.

A Terrible Privilege

Jeff's ministry remains dedicated to the military community, to those with shared combat experience, whose trauma from war requires empathy to make the connection of the case for Christ. He remains uniquely suited to minister to exactly that community. Jeff has walked into rooms full of warriors who carried the heavy burden of war with them. But those warriors were willing to talk to him in that moment. "Everybody knew me, what I'd been through, what my reputation is. Because of that, I had the honor of hearing stuff that most chaplains, most counselors, would take years to get to [hear]."

Jeff calls it a terrible privilege. "I use both those words very sincerely. It is terrible to help bear those burdens and hear those stories. I wish nobody on the planet had to hear those stories. I wish that nobody on the planet *had* those stories. But it is an incredible privilege at the same time. God has given me this terrible privilege. I cherish it. But I wouldn't want anybody else on the planet to have to go through what I've gone through to get there."

Jeff makes sure these soldiers know that God understands the heart of a warrior. During his deployments as chaplain, he would hand out Psalm 91 cards and memorabilia to guys who were not believers. Amid the violence and battles and combat, Jeff wanted these men to know: God understood.

*   *   *

God anoints us for every chapter, every season we are in. Jeff's extraordinary experience in combat, coupled with his divine assignment to minister, has rendered him life-changing for everyone in his ministry, his flock. He's life*saving*; the eternal life promised believers awaits all who have been brought to Christ. By helping warriors to believe on Jesus, he is changing earthly lives as well—helping to heal and restore the brokenhearted, those valorous warfighters who feel the weight of combat so deeply on their spirits. Now they, too, can feel the peace that surpasses all understanding.

Jeff views himself as a vessel for God's works here on Earth; I see him as a giant of faith who has been called to a divine purpose with generational impact. The gentle authority that flows from Jeff seals his impressive command of biblical teachings, history, and scripture. His inspiring story is completely unique—the experience of a combat imprint that prepared him perfectly for his ministry. His consecutive anointings for the Ranger Regiment and ministry enabled him to cultivate a very specific flock with very specific needs.

In the most ferocious of battles, amid historic loss, Jeff surrendered to God's will and was transformed by a peace that surpasses all understanding. His fellow warriors felt his peace, and wanted it too—and have all since come to Christ. His ministry now serves those brave warriors who endure the unthinkable for our freedoms, who fight for God and country together, who now rest easy at night knowing their souls are headed for heaven, and their earthly walk is guided by Jeff.

For I am convinced that neither death nor life, neither angels nor demons, neither the present nor the future, nor any powers, neither height nor depth, nor anything else in all creation, will be able to separate us from the love of God that is in Christ Jesus our Lord.

—ROMANS 8:38–39

A US UH-60 Black Hawk helicopter flying
over Mogadishu, Somalia, in September 1993.

Jeremiah Wilber, retired 18 Zulu contractor, 2021.

Jeremiah Wilber's mother, Louise "Mountain Lamb" Wilber.

3

Today Is a Good Day to Die

Sergeant First Class/
18 Zulu Jeremiah Wilber,
US Army Green Beret (Retired)

Ever since Jeremiah Wilber was a child, he knew Jesus. Growing up on and around the Fort Peck American Indian Reservation in Montana, he knew the Creator. Embracing the arduous lifestyle of his cowboy and Native community, at a young age Jeremiah was an integral part of the family's identity and activities. He was raised to be independent, capable, strong, honorable, faithful, and connected under the loving care of his parents, by which each day there were rich life lessons to learn.

As far back as he can remember, Jeremiah had developed a way to deal with fear. Under his breath, he would say a self-generated string of made-up words over and over. As he grew older, the special phrase maintained its comfort for him in intense situations. From enduring violence outside his community in Montana and in gang-ridden neighborhoods in Las Vegas, during his world champion martial arts competitions, and throughout his multiple tours of duty during Operation Iraqi Freedom as a US Army special operator, Jeremiah would repeat his seemingly meaningless phrase when he needed courage and resolve.

Until one day in 2005, in the thick of a raging firefight in Iraq, Jeremiah learned what that phrase actually meant.

Apache Cowboy

Warrior blood runs through Jeremiah's veins. On his Apache mother's side, his grandfather served as a machine gunner in the US Marine Corps, earning a Silver Star during the Korean War, which is the third-highest military decoration for valor in combat. His paternal grandfather enlisted in the US Navy at sixteen and drove assault boats in the Pacific Theater during World War II and was subsequently highly decorated. His father served in the US Army, a powerful figure in his National Guard uniform at home with the family. Growing up in the rugged wilderness of Montana, while surrounded by men like Jeremiah's father, had a huge influence on Jeremiah's life. It was instilled in Jeremiah that he never quit or ask for help in any way, never let anybody down, and never let anybody see him down.

An Apache philosophy also became part of the fabric of his being: "The other side of my nature, the Native side, was best expressed by my mother saying to me and my siblings many times: *Today is a good day to die.*" Jeremiah's mother wasn't being fatalistic or wishing for death by using those words. She lived her life so that she was prepared to meet the Creator. She was right with the Creator. Right with her family. She meant no matter what happened to her, she was ready for it. "And she wanted us to live our lives with that same spirit."

It reminds Jeremiah of Isaiah 54:17: *No weapon formed against you shall prosper.* "To me, that meant that you can do something to my physical being to harm me, but you can't really do damage to *me*, because I belong to God," Jeremiah explained. "I also heard her tell me that she loved me; I heard that a lot and her expression of her love always motivated me. It did the same for my brothers and my sister."

The application of this approach revealed itself early on. At a young age, Jeremiah was exposed to people getting seriously hurt and dying—getting bucked from horses, having accidents with tractors and other equipment. Seeing this drove home his mother's point about being right with the Creator.

Who was the Creator? "My mom's mom and my mother told me stories about how the Creator sent his son to die on a tree. There was this same creation story in the Bible. Seeing both sides of that and how and who we are as people, as human beings, springs from the same source was really big for me." Along with going to Christian church, Jeremiah also participated in Apache practices. In his house, they burned sage and smudge and sweetgrass. Importantly, Jeremiah saw the same values and beliefs expressed in "both places," in his Christian church and in his Apache orthopraxy.

The fundamental overlapping value was gratitude. "I was always taught that you never take something without giving back. That was our way of thanking the Creator for all He did for us." Growing up with that important concept of expressing and holding gratitude shaped Jeremiah and his practices. "Still today," Jeremiah shared, "I carry tobacco leaf in my pocket, and if I find a cool feather or a rock that I want to keep, I'll say a quick prayer and place some tobacco on the ground as an offering of thanks."

A Warrior Purpose

Jeremiah knows God created him for a specific purpose: to be a Warrior, just like all the men in his family. "I was made to be able to do what I did for a living. I don't really think that I had a choice. And knowing that what I did was aligned with what God wanted me to do enabled me to be good at it and to be happy." He enlisted in the Army in 1988 and served as a military policeman until 2009, when he went to the Special Forces Assessment section and qualified to become a Green Beret, the elite special operators with the motto *De Oppresso Liber*, "To Free the Oppressed."

Faith and his upbringing were the biggest influences on the kind of Warrior he became. "I don't think that I would have been as open-minded a Warrior on the battlefield, or understood the things that I did in training—working, fighting, and my blood, sweat, and tears alongside Afghan and Iraqi commandos." Jeremiah's faith helped shape his leadership qualities as well. The Afghan and Iraqi officers were Muslim, they appreciated and respected that Jeremiah had his God, served his God, and held a shared sense of what their role was in this life. Much of that was shaped by Jeremiah's Native influence. "When I was deployed and in danger, I wasn't scared of what was going on and didn't fear death. I understood that I conducted myself in such a way that it was a good day to die."

Before Jeremiah left home to join the Army, his mother presented him with a blanket. He kept it on his bed and it served as a reminder to him of his heritage and home. That reminder wasn't just for him. Along with the sweetgrass he kept in his truck and the tobacco he would sprinkle, he displayed outward signs of his spirituality. He shared the meaning and significance of those things with his fellow Warriors. As a leader, he was always alert to the physical, emotional, and spiritual needs of those under his charge. When a chaplain was available, he would make sure that his teammates knew. Jeremiah believed in being prepared for combat and for the worst-case scenario that could result. To live and serve so any day was a good day to die.

Being a Warrior necessarily included violence and ferocity. "Being a mixed-blood kid, even back in Montana, I had to stand up for myself against both Indian and white kids at school and outside it. So, from age three or four onward, I was fighting; my life was rough." Then at fourteen, Jeremiah and his family moved to east Las Vegas. The neighborhood was overrun with gangs, violence, and drugs. "What my Apache elders taught me and showed me about unity wasn't always lived out in the rest of my world. I did see that these Warriors were capable of extreme violence. They were capable of doing anything to fight for their family, their homeland, the country." But being a Warrior included love and protection too. Jeremiah saw his father, a white man, taken in by tribal elders and accepted just as if he was born Native. Jeremiah watched the Warriors show love, care, and nurturing, and observed them growing in those arenas too. A true Warrior was not simply violent. A true Warrior was principled, and a protector.

The Creator Giving Strength and Courage

The Warrior spirit does not render you immune from fear, however. "I can think of a hundred times when I was a kid and got scared." Through it all, Jeremiah turned back to his special phrase whenever he needed resolve or strength. Sometimes it was as simple as getting scared at a bonfire or a campfire, stepping out of the circle of light into near-complete darkness, or during hunting trips with his father. While hunting for elk when Jeremiah was around eight, his dad asked him to walk along a ridge as spotter and to give his dad a calf call if he saw any elk.

"This was bear country," Jeremiah recalled. "I'd seen them before. Grizzly bears. Mountain lions. That's a lot to be running through your head sitting on a ridge in the middle of nowhere by yourself. I was scared. I developed the habit of saying this phrase in tongues over and over and over again to help calm me, get me past the fear."

Jeremiah didn't know what the words meant, only the comfort that repeating them gave him. His mother offered one answer. "At the start, when I was young and scared, I didn't consciously come up with these words. I never did really know what it was I was saying. I'd just be scared and they'd come to me. I talked to my mother about my doing it. 'God,' she'd say. 'That's the Creator. He's just with you. Giving you some motivation.'"

Jeremiah and his siblings competed in elite martial arts competitions throughout his youth. He began relying on his phrase not just in times of fear, but to give him strength and courage when preparing for these top-tier fights. "It gave me a swagger," he said. "A confidence."

The Warrior at War

By the time Jeremiah was deployed to Iraq in 2005, he had been promoted to Military Police Squad Leader. He and his team had a number of different air and route security responsibilities; troops and matériel were constantly being moved, and it was their mission to ensure the safety of both. That sometimes meant going outside the wire to perform reconnaissance, provide escort, and establish a combat reaction force.

They also supported the US Marines, operating out of their base just outside Baghdad. They frequently received calls when those Marines were involved in gunfights, responding quickly to join the fight. "Over the radio and sometimes with just our ears, we could detect gunfire. We could see smoke. Whatever it was, we had to drive into."

As a squad leader, Jeremiah was responsible for others; he knew that he had to set the proper tone. Those incidents brought back feelings of uncertainty, the anxiety of not knowing what's next, but he understood that the others would take their cue from him. "I really tried to home in on that Warrior mentality, that attitude that today is a good day to die. I shared a bit of my faith with them."

And he relied on his training. "We have sayings in the Army, lessons we learn. We train to be prepared for surprising, aggressive action. And that doesn't mean that you have to have a hundred fighting against ten. I instilled in my guys the idea of being fearless. We had to do everything we could possibly do to be good at our jobs; not just be *aware* of what we needed to do, but to *actually* do it. You had to close that distance between you and fear. Feel it, but do what you need and have been trained to do."

The LORD is my light and my salvation—whom shall I fear?
The LORD is the stronghold of my life—of whom shall I be afraid?

—PSALM 27:1

Jesus Is Always with Me

In May 2005, any hope of Iraqi pre-election calm ended as the insurgency grew ever more violent. That month, Shia Muslims came under intensified attack by Sunni militants hoping to disrupt the Shia majority. More than 700 Iraqi civilians and 79 US soldiers died. That month's toll was the highest since the invasion began in March 2003. In 2005, a soldier in Jeremiah's company was killed and several from the platoon were injured.

One day, the fight came for Jeremiah. "We worked twelve-hour shifts and I served on the overnight rotation. I was sleeping and it was later in the afternoon. I heard a banging on my door. By the time my platoon sergeant opened up the door to my hooch, he was already telling me, 'You got to roll right now. Second squad just got hit and it's bad.'"

Jeremiah ran to rouse his team leaders, telling them "it was time to freaking roll." At the end of their shift early that morning, they had prepped everything for just this kind of urgent response. Jeremiah's guys were ahead of the Marines' Quick Reaction Force. His platoon sergeant and first sergeant both had gotten in a truck immediately and were the first on scene.

"We rolled in a few minutes behind. My guys spread out and took their positions efforting security. We assisted with medevacing out the wounded. They were kids," Jeremiah remembered. "The oldest twenty-two or twenty-three. No one was killed, but with the exception of two, everyone else was wounded, a lot of them seriously, with missing limbs. That was the first time that I was around guys that I knew really well who'd been hit like that. We interacted with these Marines a lot, and to see them injured and wounded and in all that turmoil, it hit me a little bit harder.

"I remember walking back from where all the casualties had been, leading these guys out of there to the aircraft, and walking back to my truck, feeling this anger boiling up inside me. But I also had to think about the young guys in my squad and how to keep them motivated. A few months before this, one of our guys, Joseph Graves, had been killed. And here, now, was my gunner, the guy who was Graves's best friend seeing this and taking part in this. And I was thinking, *Man, it's already been hard enough to get this kid, this gunner, to do the job his best friend was doing when he got his head blown off.*"

After the wounded were flown to the field hospital, Jeremiah and his men circled up. "We talked for a bit, and I could see we were on the same page. They were pissed too. You know you're in a war, so you know it could be you next. And we still had a job to do. We had to finish out that shift. I knew that we were fine. We had this. Then we got word of some suspicious activity near a radio tower."

They had received intel from Iraqi civilians. The tower near their FOB was protected by a hundred-foot wall, with garage door–like panels that allowed vehicles to access the equipment inside. Until that point in his deployment, the towers hadn't been the site of any fighting. They were connected to a small Iraqi village and were in an exposed area of the desert. Anyone nearby could spot them moving toward that position—a vulnerable spot to approach. Moreover, the insurgents had been dotting the roads that approached the location with IEDs. Along with the catastrophic damage those bombs could inflict, slowing and stopping vehicles was also problematic, as frequently those strikes were followed by ambushes. The towers and the covering structures offered the enemy the advantage of high ground and multiple points from which to launch an attack. Jeremiah weighed the options and developed a plan.

"I decided we should take the long way around. We went through a bunch of wadis and craziness and watermelon patches in our big trucks. As we were getting closer, I could see people moving around on top of that protective structure. There were some gun emplacements up there. And my gunner mother—a woman who was as tough as it gets—was yelling at me, and the .50-cal was going off. I remember how loud it all was. At the same time, I'm on the radio with my teammates, making a plan to hit this thing. We had to get the trucks as close as we could to a door, but far enough back that we could also pull security. We could take this thing from a kind of L shape. I was basically going to section this off so that my gunners could shoot at the west and south sides of this square building. I couldn't cover the backside with gunners, but I knew that we had to get inside from there.

"I was there with my interpreter, a really cool guy from outside Ethiopia. His face was all scarred up, and he was a Warrior from his tribe. He never carried a gun, but I always carried an extra AK-47 and I gave it to him. My Alpha platoon leader was with me, and my mother gunner stayed up on the mounted .50-cal. I had two other kids with me. As soon as I got around back there, I saw a bad guy go up. He was standing by the door. I didn't know if he was throwing something or dropped it, but I shot him. I went through the door and as that door was open, I saw a long hall to the right and to the left was an open courtyard. I told the interpreter to go right and hold down that big open area. I scanned above, and it looked as if the bad guys in those positions were already taken care of. Then me and my platoon leader went in. This was the first time I'd been inside something like that. And here's where it gets kind of blurry in my mind.

"It was kind of like I was in a flow state in which it seemed like the only thing I could hear as I'm moving through that building with the other guy on my hip, us leapfrogging one another, was the sound of my own breathing. I shot a guy through a window and saw into another room where two other guys threw down their guns.

"And the whole time what was so vivid was the sound of my breathing and the sound of those words I used to repeat to myself as a kid when I was scared. Those sounds were punctuated by gunshots. I didn't have earplugs in, and it was all so real. I don't know if I was repeating those words in my head, but I think it was out loud. And so McCutchen and I kept pressing forward and were ready to make this last corner where the two bad guys had surrendered.

"I became aware then of a different thought other than taking in everything in my surroundings. I was aware that I wasn't saying my words like I usually did. I was saying, *Jesus is always with me. Jesus is always with me.*"

Jeremiah, in an instant, realized that is what those words had meant the whole time. From a frightened little boy in the pitch-black Montana wilderness to a teenager encountering violence, from elite martial arts fights to this most dangerous battle in war—Jesus had been telling Jeremiah, *I am always with you.*

Jeremiah felt Jesus. Learning what those words meant was powerful. "Those words definitely made me feel that power and that presence." The greater realization was that Jesus had been with him not just in times of fear or needing courage, but unfailingly by Jeremiah's side his entire life.

You Are the Light

After the firefight and the bad guys had been captured, Jeremiah and his team searched and secured the rest of the buildings. It was past 2 a.m. when they headed back to their FOB. Jeremiah began communicating with the base over the radio, exchanging vital information. Seeds of doubt began creeping in amid him managing the comms. Had he imagined that's what the phrase meant?

But Jesus wasn't done with him yet.

Jeremiah shared, "All my life my mom would tell me something else. Driving along with her, if we'd go under a streetlight and it would shut off, she would say that was Jesus, reminding you that the light inside you is brighter than any light. You don't need a light; you *are* the light."

Jeremiah and the crew entered the final, serpentine stretch of desert road to their FOB, an otherwise ink-black landscape lit by high streetlights on either side. Then, right as they passed underneath, a streetlight went out.

"I can feel it. I can feel the wind on my face," Jeremiah remembered. He described the impact it had for the light to go out at that exact moment he was doubting what had happened in the firefight: "We probably should have gotten shot two or three times while in there. I don't know how we didn't. At the time, though, I remember hearing those words and a bunch of other ones. The devil, maybe, telling me that this was all bull**** and I'm just making it up.

"But when that light went out, I just felt good. That confirmed what I'd heard and what my mom had been telling me all those times. As a Christian, you're never alone. Jesus was with me."

Realizing what the phrase meant had larger consequences for Jeremiah's past too. "I see better that Jesus was *always* with me. I have greater clarity about that. Things around me are moving fast and are chaotic, but there's a soul stillness at my center."

Lightning in the Hand

Jeremiah's faith, his commitment as a Warrior, and the foundational teachings of his upbringing have continued to define his life's purpose after his military career. In 2022, Jeremiah founded War Party Ranch, a nonprofit organization dedicated to empowering female survivors of all forms of abuse. Recognizing that abuse of women was a serious problem in the Native community and elsewhere, and as a tribute to his mother's spirit, War Party Ranch takes action rather than just uttering words. As its mission statement says, "Less thunder in the mouth and more lightning in the hand."

*   *   *

Under His Wings

We are assured that Christ is with us always, to the very end. In our moments of fear, Jesus provides comfort. When we feel weak, Jesus provides strength. During times of jubilation, Jesus is there. And every minute in between, whether we feel worthy or not, Jesus has never left us. The power of His presence, unseen yet known, and the impact of His presence is a grace we receive because of how much God loves us.

Jeremiah's story is a testimony to that gift of grace, and to the power of the Holy Spirit that transcends generations, communities, and times. In the place of earthly fear or weakness, Jesus gives us His peace, which flows freely from His presence. The blood of Jeremiah's ancestor Warriors runs throughout his veins and flows in the blood of his children. He has served as a Warrior for this nation and in the Army of Christ, carrying the Spirit of God within for all to see.

The Lord your God is with you, the Mighty Warrior who saves.

—ZEPHANIAH 3:17

A formation of soldiers spell out "AMERICA" at the Great Lakes Naval Training
Station in Great Lakes, Illinois, during World War I.

PRISONERS OF WAR LABOR CO. 80.

My great-grandfather Lieutenant William Bertsch.
After he was wounded, he was assigned to serve at a POW camp
because he spoke German.

My great-great uncle PFC Joseph Lorenz, Rainbow Division, ca 1917.
He died in World War I and lies buried in France.

Lieutenant Colonel
Anthony Randall
prior to a
training jump.

Anthony and the ministry team at Fort Benning, Georgia, in 2015.

4

Pastor, Priest, Prophet, Person

Chaplain, Lieutenant
Colonel Anthony Randall,
US Army Ranger (Retired)

D r. Anthony Randall is an indomitable force for good, with an energy that lights up a room. A larger-than-life individual—and a captivating raconteur—he's highly accomplished and widely experienced. A twenty-four-year veteran of the US Army, he served as an Army Ranger, master parachutist, and Army chaplain. He earned two master's degrees in divinity and theology and a doctor of ministry degree. He's also an entrepreneur and leadership coach in the private sector, author, and a martial arts master, holding Japanese jujitsu third-degree and tae kwon do first-degree black belts, a judo brown belt, and a Brazilian jiujitsu purple belt.

But it is the simple shepherd's crook that most accurately represents his calling. Anthony keeps a life-size one in his office. It is plain yet beautiful, hand carved of wood. It was a going-away gift from the Army Ranger chaplains he supervised, representing his ministry philosophy he endeavored to ensure they carried on: to serve as shepherds to a flock. Drawing from his combat and life experience, Anthony derives four chaplain responsibilities for how best to serve as that shepherd: as pastor, priest, prophet, and person. These are his stories of each.

Leap of Faith

Anthony was a young airborne Ranger in 1999; he loved to leap out of airplanes. As a jumpmaster, he was the individual who would hang out the door to spot the landing zone and usher the parachutists out of the fuselage. Just a few years after graduating from the US Military Academy at West Point, he was working as an Army engineer in the 82nd Airborne Division and planned to go into Special Forces selection, with his eye on being a Green Beret. "My *eye* on," Anthony laughed, "How ironic!"

While on a routine training jump, the retina in one of his eyes detached during the parachute fall and required surgery. His commander was forced to deliver bad news: he was no longer physically capable of being a paratrooper. He was being sent to Korea instead of getting the opportunity to qualify as a Green Beret.

Anthony was angry. He was angry at the Army, angry at the leadership within it, and angry at God. The thought of having his dreams derailed felt deeply unjust. But his fellow officers went to bat for him—they knew he deserved the opportunity to qualify. He was one of very few Ranger jumpmasters in the unit, he had just returned from a six-month deployment to Egypt, and he was newly married. "It was by the grace of God that three of the other officers I worked with in the unit stood up for me," Anthony said. "They convinced the commander to keep me around. That didn't guarantee that I'd stick around much longer. So, for my last two years in the military, I spent most of my time thinking about what I could [do] to make sure that this part of my life ended well."

That part of his life did end well. At the age of twenty-seven, in 2001, he left the US Army and entered the corporate world. He quickly adapted to civilian life. He got a job in the private sector working for a Fortune 100 company and felt like he'd succeeded in reassembling all the pieces of an inchoate dream. He went to bed every night feeling like life was good for him and his wife.

Including one particular night in October 2002, which changed his life's trajectory more than his eye injury did. "It was two o'clock in the morning. My wife woke me up because I was laughing in my sleep." She asked Anthony what was so funny.

Then Anthony was suddenly overcome. He felt compelled to ask her, "Did the Holy Spirit say something to you?"

He shared further: "And you have to understand this: my wife has a very good gift of discernment. And it was true that He had spoken to her." When Anthony asked her what He said, she answered that the Holy Spirit told her that Anthony was supposed to go back into the military.

Anthony knew in that moment, with utter and immediate conviction in a clear direction sent from God, that he was going to do it. But not as an engineer. As a chaplain. "And," Anthony said with a laugh, "if you were to talk to any of my buddies from West Point, or any of the guys that knew me when I was a young lieutenant, they would agree on this: I was not chaplain material!"

The Spirit of Joy

Anthony knew it would be culture shock to go back into the Army, especially as a chaplain, but he and his wife felt the Holy Spirit. They knew what to do and had no questions about it. "People comment to me about what an amazing decision that was that I made," Anthony said. "I tell them, 'No.' At twenty-seven, that was the first time in my life that I one hundred and ten percent bought into Jesus Christ and said, 'Whatever Your will is, Lord, let it be done.'"

Jeff and his wife sold everything they owned and moved back to Denver, going from making six figures a year to less than $20,000 while Jeff went to seminary for three years. But they never missed paying a bill. "God always provided for us."

After seminary, Anthony was deployed to Iraq for a fifteen-month tour as a chaplain, followed by six more deployments with special operators in Iraq and Afghanistan. During those intense combat deployments, Anthony realized exactly how he needed to minister to these special operators. "Those experiences helped me see that there was a need for a holistic approach—spiritual, relational, mental, physical, the whole bit—to being of service to these guys. But most importantly, I used the gospel."

Anthony also used the gifts God had given him, knowing he was fully equipped for the calling God had placed on his heart. And it was delivered through—and received with—joy. "When I reflect back on that night of the dream and my laughter, scripture reminds us in Romans V, and also Philippians IV, to take joy in our suffering," Anthony said. "It's in joy that we build perseverance, in perseverance we build character, and in character we build hope in the saving grace that we have in Christ. My call to ministry was through joy, through laughter, through humor. Our family went through some very difficult things in full-time ministry; I went through some difficult things in combat. But that call was in joy."

The vibrance of Anthony's energy, the light I saw in his eyes as he told me about God's calling on him to ministry and his return to the military was radiant. His spirit of joy was infectious.

A Chaplain's Roles

Anthony described the four roles of a chaplain, and how he learned over time how to perform each role better and better—by meeting his soldiers where they were. "You've got to be a Ranger to the Ranger, a Green Beret to the Green Beret, a soldier to the soldier, whatever the case may be. Sometimes people need a pastor; they need someone who can preach and teach God's word, and need someone who can provide pastoral care and counseling. Other times they need a prophet. It's a privilege to serve as a priest. And then over time, you get to be a person."

Anthony lit up. "So that's why I love doing jiujitsu. That's why I love jumping out of airplanes. I tell guys all the time, 'Hey, if I choke you out today, I'll pray for you. If you choke me out, who you gonna go tell you choked out a broke old man who wears glasses?!' I mean, come on, really?" We both dissolved into laughter. Believe me, Anthony is *not* a broke old man.

Pastor

The most powerful pastoring sometimes occurs for the unlikeliest members of the flock. During one Iraq deployment, one of the special operators in Anthony's unit was seemingly made of steel—on the outside. As Anthony put it, "He was tough as nails. I started working out with him in the gym and doing CrossFit, and we built a relationship. He actually came to my chapel service one time. That night, I was preaching on Psalm 31:14–16. Psalm 31:15 says, *My time, Lord, is secure in Your hands. Save me from my enemies. Make Your face shine on me and show Your unfailing love.*"

The operator never came to chapel again. But then seven or eight months later, toward the end of their deployment, Anthony was in the mess hall eating. All of a sudden, the operator came up and dropped his plate on the table in front of him. "And he was a big dude," Anthony said. "And he sits down. And I'm like, 'What's up, man?' He responds, 'My time is in your hands.'" Anthony immediately got the scripture reference.

But then the operator started repeating it. He said the phrase four or five times. So Anthony asked him, "What's up, brother? What's up with 31:15?"

The operator told Anthony he had only come to one chapel service, on what was his fifteenth deployment. And it was the chapel service that saved his life.

The operator shared that his regular missions were either done solo for days at a time or with just one other person. He told Anthony, "You have no idea how much fear I faced leaving the gate every day." He added, "The only thing that kept me steady and focused on my mission—and operating in faith that I could do my mission and not in fear—was that I would say to myself, *My time is in Your hands. God, my time is in Your hands. My time is in Your hands. My time is in Your hands.*"

Anthony was overcome. "He came to *one* chapel service."

Anthony learned an important concept in ministry over time: "I don't care who comes to church, I don't care if there's five hundred people, if there's five people, I'm going to share with them the same message. I'm going to give them the same intentional preaching and teaching of the Word and pastoral care, *because the most important people that were supposed to come to that service are the people that came to your service.*"

For that one operator, attending one church service saved his life in Iraq. In that very divine appointment hearing Anthony preach Psalm 31:15, he absorbed the Word of God in the most effective way for him in that moment. He heard it, and was transformed by it. He was able to conduct his missions from a position of faith, not fear.

"That's the pastor part of my role as a chaplain," Anthony added. "Preaching God's word and helping people take God's word and internalizing it."

The *way* Anthony pastors to warriors is just as important as *when* they hear his teachings. Anthony leads a weekly men's Bible study with men from around the country. He was leading them in a discussion about a psalm of David's. "David talks about music from the choir master," Anthony said. "Do you think that he was just humming along, 'Please have mercy on me'? 'Oh, dear God my enemies . . .'? This dude cut off other dudes' heads! He stabbed people in the face.

"So I asked the group how many of them have ever prayed with anxiety, prayed with fear, psychologically shaken. *That's* when you really know how to pray. It doesn't look right in a church on a Sunday. But that's the way that Jesus prayed in the Garden of Gethsemane. Jesus sweated blood!"

Anthony paused. Then he added, "Prayer doesn't always look clean and crisp like you may see on a Sunday morning. Prayer is just bringing yourself to God."

It was rewarding for Anthony to pastor that message to those elite men, those special warriors who exist in raw intensity and face physical and spiritual battles beyond description. Not only did Anthony meet them where they were, but he brought David to them as *he* was, an elite operator just like them. The clear divine timing of Anthony's pastoral assignment is underscored as well by the operator in Iraq. That brave warrior was operating from a place of pure faith and perfect timing in the middle of combat, going out on those missions, declaring before God that his time was in His hands. That is what a psalm looks like in the application of a warrior.

Priest

Presiding over sacraments and Christian ceremonies is an honor for chaplains, even if they are sometimes shocked by who requests it. En route to another deployment with special operators, Anthony met a group of guys at the airport who were traveling to the same deployment. One of the guys asked Anthony what he did, and Anthony explained he was a unit chaplain. "He screwed up his face and said to me—first thing he ever said to me—'I hate chaplains. They're all a******s. And you're an a****** too. And, by the way, I'm an atheist.'" Anthony roared laughing. "I'm thinking that we've got forty-eight hours to travel together so that we can get to a combat zone. Well, things got off to a real good start!"

Though no one thought it was so at the time, providentially, their flight got delayed. They were going to have to spend the night in the city together. Then they were delayed even more. The group spent the entire time together, sharing meals and stories.

Finally, they were dropped off at their deployment location. As they were walking into their headquarters, the individual looked at Anthony and said, "You know what? You're not as much of an a****** as I thought you would be." Anthony laughed. "I said to him, 'Well, I'm glad that we gained some ground together!'"

The men kept spending time together during deployment. And eventually, after countless hours doing CrossFit workouts (and even joining Anthony's fantasy football league), they were cemented as friends. Then time passed, years passed.

On Anthony's very last deployment, the same group of guys from that same unit were there. A Godwink. When Anthony arrived, "They were super excited," he remembered. Then the men shared something incredible: "They had joined a Bible group. They had accepted Christ and had become Christians." From atheists and downright hostility to friendship and accepting salvation through Christ—what a cause for celebration!

Moreover, it was a very special week. It was the beginning of Lent, the week of Ash Wednesday. In advance of that, Anthony had special ashes prepared with palm branches and olive oil from Jerusalem. "And you need to understand," he tells me, "I'm a Methodist by trade, I'm a pretty low-liturgy guy. I'm like, rock and roll and raise your hands. But I enjoy liturgy."

Deployments, according to Anthony, were like the 1993 movie *Groundhog Day*. Every day looked the same, smelled the same, was the same. Thus it was important to Anthony to bring the Christian calendar to the troops; being able to celebrate spiritual days like Easter, Lent, Epiphany, Advent, and Christmas was a reminder of God's grace and His plan for them. And a way to bring deeply rooted joy and grounding to the troops during the exhausting repetition.

So, putting aside his rock and roll, Anthony decided to do a twenty-five-minute practical message for Ash Wednesday to ensure the warriors had their special worship. "That guy who had called me out came to this beginning of Lent service. I will never forget the sacred moment of putting the ashes on his forehead, and seeing the peace of Christ in his eyes for the first time."

Several years after that, the operator called Anthony and asked him to officiate his wedding. Anthony did. Now every Christmas season, when Anthony and his wife put up the Christmas cards they receive, one of his favorite moments is receiving the card from the operator and his wife, now with children, raising them in a house that serves the Lord.

"Seeing all that happen is part of playing the role of a priest to these men and women," Anthony said. Although the men got off to a rocky start, Anthony showed up in exactly the right way for those men and that operator. Simply as himself, a member of their team, consistently modeling for those men what loving Christ looks like—and more importantly, what being loved by Christ looks like. It is complete and unconditional. After accepting Anthony, one by one they accepted Christ. God used Anthony as the perfect vehicle to bring them to Christ. The gravitas of Anthony's generational impact on these warriors—saving their souls—is embodied in the honor of serving as priest on the most important day of that former atheist's life.

Prophet

Anthony emphasized the importance of the prophet role. "I've had to speak up for many soldiers who have been marginalized or oppressed by their commands many times because they're females or they're minorities, and was able to speak truth to power and hold the line and be the moral compass for a leadership team. I have no problem speaking prophetically and truthfully to people. I don't care if you're a private or you're a four-star general; I will tell you straight up what the deal is."

Anthony has done a lot of racial reconciliation ministry. During the Ferguson, Missouri, riots of 2014–15, he pastored the congregation at Fort Benning. He was also good friends with the Gospel Service pastor. The Gospel Service building had been shut down for renovations. "That just blew my mind," said Anthony. "This is in the middle of [the] Ferguson riots. No one would lift a finger to help him find a place for their congregational worship.

"I think it was very prophetic that in the midst of all this disruption, and all this racial violence and tension, he and I blended our two services together. We took a majority-white contemporary worship congregation, and a historically black congregation, and we put them together. We had our worship bands integrate together, so that it wasn't a 'we do your worship on one Sunday, and then we do my worship on the next one' kind of thing. No, you guys are gonna worship together."

The richness of the blessing was in the sermons themselves. Anthony and the Gospel Service pastor had two rocking chairs that they set onstage. "And we would team teach," Anthony explained. "We would preach the sermon together through conversation. And it was so cool to do that, to have this prophetic voice showing this is what the church should look like."

The blended service and team pastoring went on for the next three or four years. The joined congregations celebrated Easters together and Christmases together, with these special services co-pastored. Even during the summers, they would hold a big outdoor service with baptisms and barbecue.

The impact lasted far beyond those years. After a while, the congregants decided to maintain the integrity of some of their individual worship traditions and returned to different buildings. But they all maintained the relationship and the unity of one large congregation. "Even after he and I left those congregations, some of those traditions went on," Anthony shared. "And we would have people go to their chapel service and then have folks come to our chapel service."

The power of Anthony's determination changed history for those churches.

Anthony is passionately committed to doing the hard, right thing. It's the same driving force and ethos that make special operators and warfighters of all kinds so deeply special. His unique breed of military chaplain—rooted in Christ and raised in the Ranger ranks—enabled him to serve far beyond his own flock and make a historical difference in countless lives.

Person

The last of the four main roles a chaplain plays is arguably the most simple, yet sacred. A man among others. "I have a very good friend who, to this day, is not a Christian," Anthony began. "I've tried to share the gospel with him now for fifteen years."

Anthony and the operator went through some very difficult times overseas, with guys being killed in action, dealing with tough stuff back home with families, family issues. They have a very special bond, forged through fire in combat and home front stressors over the years.

Then one night they were both hanging out at his house when they were home from deployment. "I'll never forget this," Anthony said. "We would occasionally get together on the weekend and have a fire out in the backyard, have a cigar and some bourbon. My buddy is just very stoic, looking into the fire; I mean he didn't even look at me. Then out of nowhere he asked, 'Do you know why we're sitting here right now?' And I was like, 'Yeah, cuz it's Friday night, and we're smoking cigars and drinking bourbon, bro.' He shook his head. 'No, that's not why you're sitting here right now.' And I said, 'Okay, why am I sitting here right now?'

"And he said, 'The only reason you're sitting here right now on my back porch is because you wanted to be my friend before you ever tried to be my chaplain.'

"And that's what Jesus did," Anthony said. "Jesus met the woman at the well where she was, and he didn't condemn her. He said, 'Just go sin no more.' I think the older you get, hopefully, the more we understand God's grace. Every story that I see what Jesus is doing, he meets people where they're at."

That is what Anthony has always tried to do. He's always tried to bring a relationship to the ministry, to build a connection with each member of his flock. The flock has only grown in numbers while maintaining the same intimacy. "To this day," Anthony said, "I have guys reach out, spouses reach out. We have had those ongoing relationships for the last eighteen years."

And Jesus has met Anthony where he's been. "In combat, at war, you're surrounded by death. We had to deal with death. I've zipped up body bags of friends, guys who were in my chapel service twelve hours before alive and well. I've buried two very good friends in Arlington. One of them was my platoon sergeant when I was first deployed as a young guy. Later on, I was his chaplain. The other one was a very good friend, a brother in Christ in our congregation who was killed in a crazy accident.

"One of the hardest things I've ever done is stand back home at a door with a commander and ring that doorbell. A spouse opens that door and the commander makes his announcement of why we're there. I've had spouses collapse in my arms. I've had them slam the door in my face, refuse to let us in. I've listened to children whimper and cry, not really understanding that their daddy's not coming home."

After a pause, Anthony continued. "It was on my first deployment in Iraq when I really started wrestling with these things. I read a very powerful book by Dr. John Swinton. He teaches at the University of Aberdeen in Scotland. It was called *Raging with Compassion: Pastoral Responses to the Problem of Evil.* And, in the midst of combat, not only did I find my soldiers, but me, asking *Why?* With all my theological education and depth going into this, I found myself going, *What? Why? Why did he have to die? Why did that event have to happen?*

"What I found out theologically was that you can wear yourself out if you keep asking why evil exists. That's just one of those metaphysical questions that we will never answer satisfactorily. But I do know this for sure: evil exists.

"And I also know this for sure: God's already defeated it. Satan was defeated at the cross and through the resurrection of Jesus Christ. But Satan still has the power to destroy God's creation. Satan can't destroy God, so who does he try to destroy? He tries to destroy the *Imago Dei.* He tries to destroy what He created in His own image."

Those soldiers in Anthony's flock, those humans so infinitely loved by God, come to Anthony with those big whys. "I can't answer people's why. And this is what I learned from Dr. Swinton. The one question I can answer is how: *How* do you respond to evil and *how* do you resist evil?"

Anthony is honest about wrestling personally with those fundamental questions too, and how he works through those difficult times. "I think of the traumas over the years.

I lost eighteen friends who were killed in action. I wear these bracelets to honor each of them. I've got one private moment I dedicate to one of them every month of the year. On those nights, I sit out on the back patio, I have a cigar, and I drink a glass of bourbon. My kids, my wife, they know that's my time. And I'm there honoring and remembering. So, I think that's how I worked through those difficult times and deal with those difficult, and very human, questions."

The Anthony as person, the man among men, is uncompromisingly earnest and authentic. The impressively large yet intimate community he has gathered around him is a testament to who he is as a man—and it's that man that these operators connect with. Their chaplain shares their same anguish over loss, anguish over evil, and life challenges those warriors face. It's that common thread that pulls everyone close, under the gentle guidance of their shepherd, who knows just how to comfort them in the ways of Christ.

Salvation is found in no one else, for there is no other name under heaven given to men by which we must be saved.

—ACTS 4:12

A Brother in Christ at Christmas

Anthony shared a very special Christmas experience from Iraq. One Christmas Eve he had gone out to one of their smaller stations to minister, a good distance from the main base. "I felt like that traveling Methodist pastor of the eighteenth century, going from town to town!" he said, laughing. On the sacred, joyful morning of the following Christmas Day, he was set to lead the worship service. He watched from the front of the chapel as the warriors came in for the service, and Anthony prepared to begin. "And then this Iraqi walks in—a big, big guy," Anthony said. "And all eyes lock on him, even though we're on a secure compound. He walks right up to me."

"And what do you think happens?" Anthony asked.

I was on the edge of my seat—a thousand answers flashed through my mind.

"He says to me, 'I'm a Christian. I want to celebrate Christmas with you and your soldiers. This is the safest place for me to worship.'"

Anthony welcomed him.

"This brother in Christ, who didn't look like us, didn't speak our language the same way or as well, didn't do so many things that we did, had the courage to walk into that Christmas service to worship with us. And we worshipped together."

Anthony thought at that time, and has reflected often since, how we live in a world where we are barraged with myopic, divisive judgment and thinking, especially on social media. "I'd see him later around the compound, and he worked there on the outpost. It reminded us that God is no respecter of person. And in this world today, where everything is so divisive, this was just an awesome example of how Christ can help us break some of those barriers down."

I can think of no greater gift than serving as a refuge for worship, a safe place for a person to declare his faith in Jesus Christ. The honor of being that place for this man, of presiding over his worship alongside so many different individuals united by their acceptance of Jesus, is enormous. Outside the safety of the American compound, that man was not safe to practice Christianity—so geographically close to the birthplace of Jesus himself, on the day we celebrate His birth. God blessed Anthony and the warriors serving on that base with helping to bring that brother in Christ home, to fellowship with freedom. I pray that man of faith is safe, his family blessed, his household boldly serving the Lord each and every day.

A Christmas to Remember in the Church of Community

One of Anthony's favorite Christmases was unconventional. But it was hallmarked by two of his prominent traits: fellowship and resolve. He was still with the special operations unit, between deployments, and one Christmas Eve was walking around their housing unit. He could see that a lot of families weren't going to go to church that day. Operators tend to operate in black and white, with very little gray in their lives. An idea sprang to mind. He knew just what they needed.

After floating the idea by his wife, Anthony recruited another chaplain buddy of his to help, and they organized a wonderful Christmas worship and celebration right in their own home.

Ultimately, around seventy-five special operators with their families all came over. Anthony preached the Word, and then everyone enjoyed a delicious potluck, talking and laughing and enjoying themselves. "We had a fire pit going outside and music playing, guys smoking cigars, kids running around the place. That was one of the most wonderful Christmases I remember spending back home," Anthony said. "Opening up our place, creating a place that was safe, spiritually, psychologically, and physically for people who might not have otherwise gone and worshipped anywhere."

This special operator family was able to worship and rejoice, to celebrate the birth of Jesus and celebrate their love for each other in a safe place for them. Anthony met these warriors as a man among men, as their pastor. He saw the needs for fellowship and for safety. Their chaplain brother in combat made what can be one of the most challenging days of the year for warriors the joyful celebration it should be. Anthony's servant's heart is matched only by his extraordinary gift for shepherding what God put on his heart that night long ago in Colorado.

The Shield of Faith

Anthony knows that he wasn't lucky to survive combat during his multiple deployments: He was blessed. The shield of faith protected him. Before he deployed for the first time, his father prayed over him, declaring the words from the Second Book of Kings. In those passages, Elijah and his servant are surrounded by an enemy who wants to kill them. Through God's intervention, he and his servant escape what seems to be certain death.

"When my dad prayed that over me, I really felt the Holy Spirit, a covering of the Holy Spirit in a powerful way. And so, I prayed that prayer, through every combat deployment I've ever went on: '*Lord, surround me with your horses and chariots of fire, the heavenly hosts, deny and disrupt and destroy the enemy's plans against me and bring us victory against the enemy.*'"

Anthony has had multiple experiences in combat where he has witnessed evil all around, and he has remained unscathed. "I have literally missed IEDs blowing up in the vehicle in front of me," he shared. "Once, I was walking back to my tent and an Iranian rocket that was being used by the militias in Iraq came in and hit our command tent. The Iraqis had pinpointed our commanders, and I was walking back with our sergeant major and watched our tent go up."

71

Anthony raised his eyebrows and shrugged before going on. "The only reason I did not go back after lunch that day early was because my vehicle was in the motor pool and I'd left my laptop down there and I had to go get it. Had I gone through my normal routine that day, I would have been sitting in there on my cot. When I walked in later to survey the damage, there was shrapnel, pieces a couple inches big on my cot, on my couch, and hammered into the plywood just above my desk. I would have been shredded.

"That's the shield of faith. That was always my prayer: *Lord, surround me with Your horses and chariots of fire, the heavenly hosts.*"

* * *

Anthony is a walking blessing, the kind of man who carries an earned joy with an unmatched empathy. His disciple's heart is clear, spreading the Word and Christ's love while also loving others in the unconditional, selfless way Christ Himself modeled. On the complicated journey navigated by those who serve in combat, processing prior events during post-deployment phases is equal in import to the combat experience itself.

Having Anthony as a chaplain, or even just a friend, a fellow combat veteran who shepherds his flock in the precise ways they need, is a gift. At times pastor, priest, prophet, and person, Anthony's priceless purpose is knowing what these warriors need, and when. The greatest gift, perhaps, is Anthony showing others they can live with joy too. They are approved and worthy of joy just as they are. Not because of who they are, but *Whose* they are.

> *Be shepherds of God's flock that is under your care,*
> *watching over them—not because you must, but because you*
> *are willing, as God wants you to be; not pursuing dishonest gain,*
> *but eager to serve; not lording it over those entrusted to you,*
> *but being examples to the flock.*

—1 PETER 5:2–3

Lockheed P-38s "Lightnings"
in formation over Yugoslavia
in 1944.

The pilot and copilot assigned to the Black Aces of Strike Fighter Squadron (VFA) hold up a potent symbol of freedom while flying over Afghanistan in 2009.

My two favorite pilots, who happen to be my cousins!

5

Eyes in the Sky

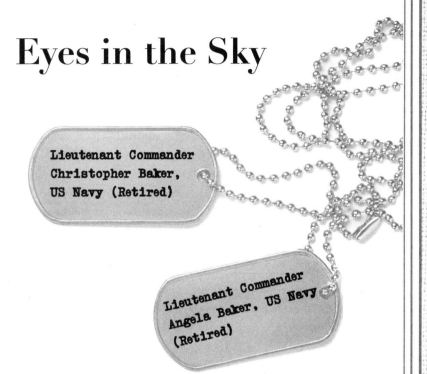

Lieutenant Commander
Christopher Baker,
US Navy (Retired)

Lieutenant Commander
Angela Baker, US Navy
(Retired)

W hile I didn't make the height cutoff to be a fighter pilot, I had the next-best thing: fighter pilots in my family. Lieutenant Commander Chris Baker (or just "Baker" to me) has always been larger-than-life, the funniest guy in the whole world—and because our moms are cousins and were lifelong best friends, Baker has been like a big brother to my sisters and me. Accompanying him to flight school were my vicarious dreams and our family's utmost pride. But then the impossible happened: there was an even *more* amazing pilot in his flight school. A United States Air Force Academy graduate, more accomplished, brighter, smarter, a better pilot, and way better-looking. Lucky for us, Baker married her.

Lieutenant Commander Angie Baker thus became a member of our family, and the US Navy gained a husband-and-wife aviator duo. While they flew different aircraft in different squadrons, with different missions, they shared a call sign: Shake 'n' Bake.

They shared something else as well, the most fundamental thing: their faith and their prayers for the soldiers below.

The Slow and Tangled Road That Led Me Straight to You

The story of Chris and Angie really begins before they met, when they both decided to become naval aviators. Chris freely admits his path was relatively easy—and unorthodox. "I entered the Navy thanks to an International Beers of the World party," he told me in all seriousness. "It's a modern miracle that I was there talking with a guy about how my life sucked. He told me I should quit my job and join the military. I handed in my two-week's notice, went to a recruiter, and two weeks later I had a flight slot."

Angie's path was the complete opposite, including a series of stalls and restarts. "I had many nos along the way to becoming a pilot. No initially to getting into the Academy. Going to prep school first. As a pilot—no to flight physical, no at the Academy with the number of pilot training slots cut, no trying for a slot on active duty, no initially to being released by the Air Force to go to the Navy. I had to keep pushing, trying, and fighting. So many to count, which is also why it is so mind-blowing how easy it was for Chris. I thought it wasn't going to happen—and God made a way."

She also kept praying. Angie was very close with God and prayed often. She prayed her whole life to become a pilot, and when she was in the thick of the challenges and the nos, she didn't understand and felt frustrated. "I cried a lot!" she said.

But with the perspective she holds today, she knows it was all part of God's plan. "I learned to have patience and faith in Him," she told me. "And He provided me with more than I was even asking for. God provided me my future husband and experiences that I could only dream of. God made that happen for me through prayer."

Angie became a navigator, but she still wanted that coveted seat at the controls. And God was still at work in her life. One of her Air Force Academy classmates had made the switch to the Navy and guided her how to interservice transfer. Finally, her prayers were answered.

Unlike their pre-pilot paths, once they started flying, Angie's career shot forward and Chris's training stalled. "Mine was slow and tangled, and Angie's was fast. But that meant that we wound up in advanced pilot training together. She was a way better pilot than I was, let's be honest," Chris declared. "She graduated top of our class. She was a lieutenant, and I was an ensign. So she outranked me. It wasn't until about nine months later that we started dating. I'm just glad that she didn't shoot me down!"

God Bless Us Apart, God Bless Us Together

In the military, even living together as husband and wife was a challenge. When they were first married, Angie was flying with a squadron in Hawaii, and Chris was stationed on Whidbey Island, off the coast of Washington state. They were barely seeing one another, with one of them flying aboard an aircraft carrier while the other was a stateside flight instructor, plus other assignments around the globe. They were in different squadrons, flying different planes (Angie the P3C, Chris the EP-3), and flying different missions. It took a deployment for them to be in the same room! They were able to meet in Bahrain for a short time, enjoying the kind of time together that many couples might take for granted (like shopping—though for them, it was rug shopping in a souk). They knew at the time how significant that was. "That we would even be able to see each other on deployment was a blessing. Spending time together was really special," Chris said.

Chris and Angie flew different variants of the Lockheed EP-3 aircraft. It is an electronic signals reconnaissance aircraft. Known by the acronym ARIES (Airborne Reconnaissance Integrated Electronic System), the EP-3 variants have signals intelligence (SIGINT) capabilities. Those onboard assets enable the crew to intercept signals, communications between people, or other electronic transmissions. In times of war or peace, intelligence-gathering is vital to future planning and in-the-moment strategy. The role of the EP-3 in overall defense strategy was so paramount during the operations in Iraq and Afghanistan that each day when the president was briefed he was notified where all the EP-3s were located. Though relatively few in number, that aircraft was integral to our nation's safety. The pilots and crew—linguists, cryptographers, and technicians—are among the many heroes of our armed forces.

While they were separated by duty, they were connected by prayer. And they had each experienced just how powerful prayer was. One moment in particular for Chris revealed the real, immediate power of prayer. It occurred during an intense simulation of how to endure being captured by the enemy while in Survival, Evasion, Resistance, and Escape (SERE) training. "I was getting beat up. Then I was interrogated," Chris described. "I was in a really stressful physical position and my legs were on fire from the pain. My interrogator asked me, 'Do you believe in God?' I told him 'Yes, sir.' Then, mocking me, he asked, 'Why don't you ask God to take the pain away?' So, I did that. I prayed silently, *'Dear Lord, please, please, take the pain away.'*

"As soon as I spoke those words, the pain was gone. And I then felt like, *All right, game on! I can do this all day!* My whole life, being Catholic, I'd prayed. And a lot of times I prayed for outcomes. And sometimes I got the one I wanted and sometimes I didn't. And a lot of the time I prayed for things farther off in the future. But this was instantaneous. That experience reinforced the power of prayer to me. I lean on that."

Angie leans on the power of prayer too. "God bless us apart, God bless us together," she prays. Their prayers extend beyond each other. "We both continue to ask God to keep our country safe. And I know that Chris prayed with his crew. I prayed with mine."

Trust in him at all times, O people; pour out your hearts to him,

for God is our refuge.

—PSALM 62:8

Let Go and Let God

The stakes are high for aviators, especially during combat missions. They are flying planes that are not infallible. Machines break and can fail. They are shot at. The nature of that work environment plays a real role in their sense of safety and security. But faith plays the largest role.

Because Chris and Angie lead such prayerful lives, they maintain peace despite appreciating the risks. "Having prayer on the road in the Middle East was a bulwark against the uncertainty of life, the uncertainty of what's going to happen with these missions," Chris said. Most of their missions were flown at night, with heightened risks to safety, and a lurking fear of the unknown. "But there are also things that I do know," he said. "And among those are my faith in Jesus and my faith in God. And I know that I felt better, had less anxiety, because I had prayer in my life. It helped me get through it all."

Chris had faith in God's plan, and he knew what he could control himself. "Let go and let God. He has a plan. I have mine. I'm responsible for my crew, to fly the missions and come back safely, hopefully—and do it all again tomorrow."

Later on, well past the war, Chris and Angie compared logbooks and realized they were both flying missions over Afghanistan at the same time. Knowing your wife was flying missions during wartime over combat zones, knowing your husband was flying missions over combat zones—each while you were doing it too—is an exceptional situation. "I might not have been fearful for myself," Chris said. "But somewhere in the back of my mind, even while flying, I had thoughts about my wife. I prayed daily for her safety."

Angie needed those prayers. In Afghanistan, she was taking incoming shots while she flew. She'd been told in preflight briefings that the altitudes at which they were flying their P-3C AIPs put them out of range of those missiles, but they learned in real time that wasn't true. During one such flight over Afghanistan, the warning system went off. She was flying with her wing commander. Training immediately kicked in and options flashed through Angie's mind in an instant: "Chaff and flares? Or evade?" Angie prayed before her missions for situations such as that. *"Lord, protect us. Lord, keep us safe. God, tell me what to do to make the right decision."*

It was a vastly different scenario than the risks she faced in other non-combat locations. But there were still major risks on those missions too.

While flying a mission off the coast of Japan, Angie's plane lost an engine over the water. She was conducting a twelve-hour overwater search mission. She prayed then that the other engine wouldn't fail. She had lives under her control, the eleven people in the back of the aircraft. That added another level of stress and worry and subject of prayers. She was aware of these risks, aware at any moment that the lives in her plane or in Chris's plane could be threatened one way or another. "But having that prayer and knowing that God was with us, if the plane was going to go down, it was going to go down," Angie said. "There was peace and comfort in knowing that we were in God's hands."

It wasn't just the crews in the planes Angie prayed for. "I remember one night flying over Afghanistan and seeing below us a major battle going on. Even from our altitude and flying at night, we could make out where caves in the mountainsides were located. We could see the muzzle flashes from weapons being fired. And that went on for a couple of nights in a row." She recognized the vastly different circumstances her fellow troops were in. "I was flying in my aircraft, reasonably comfortable. If I had to go to the bathroom, if I needed a drink of water, what I needed was there with me. We were safe. All our needs were met, we had a plan if something were to go wrong."

She knew her prayers for the warriors below were vital. "I prayed for our troops down on the ground, for their safety—and for America's success."

Chris had also been praying mightily for them. "The price those guys and gals on the ground pay is enormous. How could you not pray for them? What they do is so consequential. If you're a prayerful person, you one hundred percent are praying for the success of those boots on the ground."

In a special turn of events, Angie was able to share with ground operators that the eyes in the sky above actively prayed for them. While on base in Bahrain with another pilot, Angie spoke with some special operators about their reconnaissance flights. "They got it. They understood our role in delivering intelligence to their command group on the ground. We were their eyes in the sky. And they thanked us for being those for them," Angie recalled in disbelief. "And I said to them, 'What do you mean thank us? Thank *you*! You're the ones down there engaging in firefights.'" Then she told them she prayed for them from above. And their gratitude was profound. They knew the pilots above were fulfilling their part of the greater mission to support the operators on the ground with intel, but had no idea they were calling on God for their protection too. These warriors hadn't fathomed their eyes in the sky were also covering them in prayer.

Recaging the Gyros

Chris and Angie are committed to raising their children in church and teaching them about the power of prayer. They emphasize too that sometimes prayers are answered, and sometimes they're not—but it always turns out beautifully. God's plan enabled them to create their beautiful life as a family. "Honestly, I'm the luckiest guy in the world, probably because I married Angie so many years ago," Chris said.

This outstanding husband and wife, dual naval aviators, took a moment to reflect on God's goodness in their lives, in the countless ways God has blessed them. Through answered and unanswered prayers. They leaned on prayer in stressful and dark times: during combat, physical separation, while navigating the unknown, and in intense high-risk flight situations. They also lean on prayer to rejoice and to show gratitude to God for His favor.

Chris is used to high-altitude vantage points. "Big picture, forty-thousand-foot view, prayer is an opportunity to find true north, to interact with God. In aviation language, we call that 'recage the gyros,'" Chris said. "Pun intended: Prayer helps us stay grounded.

Faith gives me a chance to stay grounded, to destress, to focus on what's important to get the mission done—whether the mission is at home or flying in Afghanistan or Iraq."

Pilots rely on gyroscopes for orientation. For those without wings, we've likely experienced times when we feel lost or disoriented. Recaging the gyros gives pilots the opportunity to lock those gyroscopes on a fixed position and reestablish their attitudes. It's a reset, to make sure you're on the right track.

*   *   *

In the same way, God is the fixed position we lock on to. When you seek God first, and keep Him as your true north, everything else falls into place. You can rest assured that all things happening are part of His larger plan. God makes our crooked places straight and orders our steps. Even if it doesn't feel like it along the way, and you're only seeing closed doors, eventually all is revealed—God's blessings are in both answered prayers and those unanswered prayers that lead to your destiny.

These exceptional, highly decorated naval aviators encompass decades of elite training and investment by the US military into their demonstrated talents. They are the best of the best, entrusted with multimillion-dollar, classified-technology aircraft and the priceless cargo of human lives. Their specific missions in war gathered intelligence handed to the Commander in Chief every day. But by focusing on faith first, as prayerful pilots, Chris and Angie knew they could focus on their crucial jobs without fear or anxiousness. They could execute their vital missions to the utmost of their elite ability and leave their loved ones, and their brothers and sisters below, in God's hands. They were the eyes in the sky for the warriors below, covering them in prayer, as our Heavenly Father watches over us all, our "coming and going, both now and forevermore" (Psalm 121:8).

Rejoicing in hope, patient in tribulation,
continuing steadfastly in prayer.

—ROMANS 12:12

Soldiers from the "Iron Eagle" brigade bring a bit of Christmas to Camp Taji near Baghdad in December 2008.

Sergeant Jessica Harris at the Regional Counterdrug
Training Center in Washington state.

6

A Combat Medic's Courage

Sergeant First Class
Jessica Harris,
US Army (Retired)

US Army Combat Medic Jessica Harris is the kind of person you would want close by in any emergency situation—especially if you needed your life saved. Level-headed, preternaturally calm, exceptionally capable, Jessica is uniquely suited to the stressors and demands of high-intensity medical emergencies. Not only that, but with a dry wit that's always bubbling to the surface, she is likely the only medic on this planet who could make you laugh while you are losing a limb. Her faith in her abilities and her yearning to contribute where she was needed drove her to volunteer to deploy to Iraq. Finally, the opportunity came. But then came the doubts.

One night, minutes before deploying with her Army Reserve unit, the calm exterior cracked. She had asked for this—but what if she failed? Two medics had just been killed in Iraq. Her friends were dying over there. And now, lives would truly be *in her hands* in combat. The wounded would depend on her performing her job to the greatest possible degree. So she had a conversation with God. With all her might, she asked Him for strength and courage.

Then while in Iraq, after a US military convoy had been attacked with tank-piercing missiles, Jessica was called to duty, and to purpose. The lives of gravely wounded soldiers lay in her hands. And Jessica felt and knew—with unequivocal certainty—God was with her, guiding her hands.

*M*A*S*H* Beginnings

Jessica had no plans to join the Army. She didn't come from a military family. Independent and self-assured, Jessica's initial plan was to go to medical school and become a heart surgeon. Then in high school, a recruiter told her the Army would pay for all of college and medical school. "Well, that sounded awesome!" Jessica said. And she'd just be on duty in the Guard one weekend a month, two weeks a year. And just like that, trauma medicine became her specialty.

Her very first unit was a Mobile Army Surgical Hospital (MASH) unit. "Who doesn't love *M*A*S*H*?" Jessica said, laughing. "The unit literally was like that sitcom. The doctors, the nurses, it was awesome."

Sergeant Harris in 2009 while with Troop C, 1st Squadron 303rd Cavalry Regiment, explaining Entry Control Point operations to Major General Daniel Bolger, Commanding General, 1st Cavalry Division.

A Conversation with God

Jessica raised her hand to serve in combat. She volunteered to deploy to the Middle East, but her request was denied. "I was told they still needed medics to stay within the state for regular operations," she said. "I hated every minute of that. I saw all my friends deploying. I wanted to go with them and do what they were doing. I wanted to be there to help them if they got injured. Being left behind was really difficult."

Then by the time the brigade was scheduled for deployment again, she was in an aviation unit that wasn't scheduled to go downrange. "Again, I was disappointed," she remembered. "I was thinking, *I gotta go, people! It's my turn.*"

Finally, in 2008, it was Jessica's turn. She was deployed to Iraq as part of Operation Iraqi Freedom, serving as the senior medic for the 1-303 Cavalry Regiment. The all-male unit headed to premobilization training at Fort McCoy in Wisconsin, now with seven women attached to it. The training lasted a few months, and the unit prepared to deploy to Iraq. The departure time arrived. As the unit was loading up, she had a thought: *This is really happening. I'm getting what I asked for.*

The gravitas hit her. "I went back to the barracks, alone, making sure that everything was clean and everyone was accounted for. I went into a restroom. I started to cry—the first, and the only, time I cried. The weight and the pressure of my role as medic really came down on me.

"Besides having to take care of these guys, I was new to that unit, an all-male unit. I was going to, as a female, really work hard to earn their trust. I didn't have a problem with that. Once I could show them that I was tactically and technically proficient at my job, they wouldn't care about who the medic was—a man or a woman. 'Can you save us? Cool, that's all we need.' I had three other medics going and they were awesome. I also felt the pressure of being their senior medic. I had taught them things; they had taught me things, but, ultimately, I was the one responsible for what they knew and could do."

Then she thought of all those soldiers getting on the buses. They were filled with young people, and it was she who was responsible for making sure they got back home.

"That was why I went into that bathroom and cried," she said. "And I called on God, for the first time as an Army medic, for help."

Jessica's years of training and service flashed through her mind. This was go time, and she was now not only going to war, but was going to war while being responsible for an entire unit of young soldiers. "When I prayed," she said, she told God, "'If You can hear me, I need You to hear me, really hear me, on this one.'"

The real risk of sacrificing their lives was fresh on her mind. "When our brigade went on their first deployment and I was left behind and stayed back, two of my really good friends were badly injured and one was killed. And the one who was killed was a medic. I had always looked up to him. One of the injured later died, and he was a medic also. And that was really hard for our little medical community because that's not what is supposed to happen.

"Those were the things on my mind when I was praying in the bathroom—*My friends are dying.*" She could only cry out to God for His comfort in her time of pain and fear.

"I stood there in that bathroom thinking and praying," Jessica said. "You go through all these years and years of training, and it's boring half the time and you hate it. And you don't understand; things don't make sense. But all that training that the military has you do is really about developing muscle memory. And *that's* why you do these monotonous tasks over and over and over.

"So that when you're in that real-life situation, that first time, that you're not even having to think about what you're doing, because you just know how to do it. But that was my fear standing in that bathroom. Before getting on the plane, I thought, *What if I forget everything I've ever learned in the last decade? What if the sh** hits the fan, and I freeze up?* No one wants to be that person. That night in the bathroom stall, I really leaned on God and started talking to Him more."

The Army has a Combat Medic Prayer. Jessica kept a copy tucked into a small Army Bible that her aunt had given her before she deployed. "There was a line in the prayer about having the courage to step up when the time comes. And that's what I asked for, a lot of courage. And I asked for that a lot during that deployment."

Be strong and courageous. Do not be afraid; do not be discouraged,
for the Lord your God is with you wherever you go.

—JOSHUA 1:9

*　　*　　*

The Combat Medic Prayer

*Oh, Lord I ask for your divine
strength to meet the demands of
my profession. Help me to be the
finest medic, both technically and
tactically.*
*If I am called to the
battlefield, give me the courage to
conserve our fighting forces by
providing medical care to all who
are in need.*
*If I am called to a
mission of peace, give me the
strength to lead by caring for
those who need my assistance.*
*Finally, Lord, help me to take care
of my own spiritual, physical, and
emotional needs.*
*Teach me to trust in your
presence and never-failing love.*

AMEN

Courage in Combat

Though armed with that prayer, Jessica still had to wrestle with self-doubt that crept in. As she put it, "In any job, especially in the medical field, it's easy to doubt your skills and your abilities. Even though you practice things over and over, it's easy to doubt yourself. But I could never show that to anyone. I never wanted anyone to see that. So, another part of my job was to portray confidence—demonstrate an I-got-this-we're-all-going-to-be-fine kind of thing."

Then Jessica's courage under fire was tested. Six months into her deployment, they were conducting a security mission near Baghdad, heading back to Al Taqaddum Air Base. "My truck commander got an alert from a unit that was traveling in the opposite direction from us. I could hear this coming over the radio, and I had a did-I-hear-what-I-just-hear moment. This was my first call when I was going to be needed."

The other unit had been hit with an explosively formed projectile (EFP). The EFP had pierced at least one of their armored vehicles. They didn't have a medic with them, and they were looking for a nearby unit who had one. "We started racing toward them along a main road. It was dark but streetlights were on. Within a few minutes as we approached, we could see the flashes of small arms. I said a quick prayer for the other unit's safety," Jessica recalled. The unit was still taking fire. "We just keep approaching. And that moment was simultaneously the slowest and fastest of my life. Time seemed to stand still."

Her truck commander ordered her to stay in the vehicle. That was standard operating procedure; you don't want your medic jumping out and risking becoming a casualty. Medics are too vital. "That was hard for me," Jessica remembered. "I saw guys laying on the ground, and I wanted to get out there to them. I said another quick prayer that God would help me be prepared and do my job well."

The scene was secured, and she exited the vehicle along with the guys from the other vehicles in their convoy. "I'll never forget this," Jessica said. "One guy came up to me and said, 'You got this.' I didn't really know him, and we weren't good friends, but he said that." That encouragement was just what Jessica needed in that moment. A blessed messenger.

A pile of freshly dug-up dirt was in between her vehicle and the scene of the explosion. As Jessica and that same soldier approached the berm, they hesitated for a fraction of an instant. "We'd been trained to avoid walking over anything that showed any sign of having recently been dug up or looked disturbed," Jessica explained. "That was where an IED could have been buried. There was no way around it. We locked eyes for a second. Because you have to joke around with one another—it's almost a reflex action—I said, 'Well, if we go, at least we go together!' Now I think, *what a gross thing to say*, but back then we both just laughed. If you didn't have that weird sense of humor you wouldn't be able to get through some stuff."

They made it through and encountered the devastating scene. The unit had three severely wounded. One had a grave head injury. Another soldier had already been moved to another vehicle. The first injured soldier Jessica treated had a gaping wound on his left side, from his hip area about halfway down his leg. "His hamstring muscle was just blown out," Jessica said. "One of his buddies was with him, and I did what we regularly do to assess the patient initially. I started talking to him. And you should have seen the look of shock on both their faces [because] I was a woman!"

The soldiers were part of a Texas Combat Arms unit in the Texas National Guard. "Here you are in the middle of a road in Iraq after your vehicle gets hit by what is essentially a missile, and the last thing you expect to see is a woman running up to you. I think that may have made them a little nervous at first," Jessica said. She reacted with her usual resolve—and humor.

"So I said, 'Hey, you guys. You don't have your own medic, this is what you get!' I don't know if that was a comfort or not for them, but it helped me. It was clear he was in a lot of pain, and I wanted to get him comfortable as fast as possible."

Jessica carried morphine in a pouch she wore. "I reached in, and I became really aware for the first time that my hands were shaking," she said. "*Get your sh** together*, I said in my mind. *Get it together!* I'd heard stories of medics rushing and then accidentally sticking themselves with morphine." She was not going to make that mistake.

In that instant, however, all of her training kicked in. Her decade-plus of experience, her finely tuned skill set, the stoicism under pressure she was known for: it all kicked in. Her prayers were answered, and her courage poured forth. And she knew God was there with her.

"The weird thing is, I injected him, tossed the needle [aside], and it was like I'd given *myself* morphine. A wave of calm came over me. I knew that was the presence of God there with me. After that, everything, that herky-jerky fast-slow time thing, stopped. Everything proceeded fluidly. I knew what to do. I knew what questions to ask. I knew how to treat the injuries, what to tell the other soldiers, what they could do to assist me while I treated the other guys, and I just moved from one injured guy to the other.

"The rest of my squad was doing the job really well too. It was an almost textbook example of how to proceed on-site like that. I also trusted that the nonmedical guys were doing their jobs, pulling security, because we have to rely on them. I can't fight and treat at the same time; having trust in others was essential to a good outcome for everybody."

At one point, Jessica took a few seconds to assess the entire scene and realized how successful the full response was, how well every soldier was performing in the emergency. Then she heard a bunch of commotion and that drew her attention.

"I saw one of our trucks using a winch and a rope, pulling down a streetlight. I say commotion because I was hearing voices, but everybody was moving like it had all been choreographed. Everybody had a role to play, and they were doing it. It was an amazing moment of recognition. With that light out of the way, a helicopter could come in and evacuate the injured to a field hospital."

Did the three injured soldiers make it? Jessica didn't know—but she knew God was in control of the outcome. "Two of the men had horrific injuries. The soldier with the leg wound and another who had lost an arm. Those are things that aren't easy to recover from. What happened after we got them stabilized, I don't know. God put me and my crew there on that road at the right time.

"In the moment, you're so focused on doing your job and keeping them alive so they can be moved where they can receive even more intensive care. That's all I'm really thinking about. I would ask them their names and things like that to keep them calm, but after that, those names just disappeared from my mind. Only later, after the fact, did I start to wonder about what happened after they left us. As combat medics, we have to accept the fact that we can only do so much. I also think that the decision about whether or not someone lives or dies has already been made by God."

*   *   *

Jessica's prayers were answered. In the thick of battle, when lives were in her hands, she met the difficult demands of a combat medic. She was, indeed, a fine medic technically and tactically. Through the grace of God and her own determination, she showed true courage and provided medical care to those in need, successfully triaging their severe wounds and successfully conserving their fighting forces as a result. The entire unit excelled when the stakes were most high, working as a synchronous team to save their own.

And in her leaning on the Lord totally and continuously, in her trusting in His presence and in His never-failing love, Jessica ensured her own spiritual needs were met, and this ensured she blessed others. She might not have been who the soldiers expected to see, but she was an angel to them. Names might not be remembered, but the caliber of her care and the fulfillment of her duty will never be forgotten.

A Christmas Covered in Glitter, with a Star of Bullets

Jessica spent a Christmas while deployed in Iraq, with a few unexpected twists. Somehow, they had a large Christmas tree to enjoy. "I have no idea who found one in the middle of Iraq, but they did. It was left by another unit that had moved out." There was a garland on it, but the star on top was the best part. "It was an ammo belt from an M249 (machine gun). A star made of bullets!" We laughed together at that image, but then Jessica said, "The real funny story happened later."

Jessica's sweet mom was very diligent about sending thoughtful care packages. Jessica received magazines, snacks, and a bunch of other delightful things sent regularly from home. "The rest of my unit was quite jealous," Jessica chuckled. Until something came that no one wanted.

"A week or two before Christmas, I got another box. As usual, it was decorated with stickers. I was sitting in my room waiting to go to an important meeting a bit later, and mail call happens. I get the box. I've got time on my hands, so I decide to open it. I knew she was sending me a few things for Christmas. I opened it and there was a miniature Christmas tree. There were a few wrapped presents, and some cards."

It sounded lovely! "Now, you have to understand that I had on a clean uniform," Jessica told me. "We weren't scheduled to go out on an operation for a few days. I have my rifle slung over my shoulder. I decided to open one of the cards. I unsealed the envelope. AND OUT COMES A FOUNTAIN OF GLITTER! It spills all over me, my uniform, my weapon, my boots—everywhere. I looked like I just stepped out of an Iraqi strip club!"

We died laughing. "By this time, I didn't have time to change my uniform before getting to that meeting with our command staff. And I've got glitter all over my M-16! I can't let anyone see that. I grabbed some baby wipes and started trying to clean my weapon, and I can only do so much."

How did the squad react?! "Of course there were jokes about working at the 'Lake Habbaniyah strip club' (which wasn't an actual thing, of course!) but I simply explained

I had to do something on the side because getting paid as an E-6 in war wasn't bringing in enough money."

Oh my goodness how we laughed! Poor Jessica. Glitter is sort of . . . eternal. Was it ever fully cleaned up? "After lots of cleaning of my boots, room floor, and my rifle, I was mostly glitter-free after a few days, but the desert sand still remained, and every once in a while, a sparkle. You just can't get rid of the stuff!"

As a former NFL cheerleader, believe me, I'm familiar with glitter. It never fully goes away. Nor does the stigma of certain packages! I mailed a buddy in Iraq a package once from our friend group at home, and he berated me for years about it smelling like perfume (accidentally! I didn't mean to!) since he got so much teasing from the unit.

Jessica was the sparkliest soldier in Iraq, and I have no doubt the sand still glints with glitter where she opened her mom's sweet gift.

In Angels' Hands

Jessica read the Bible her aunt had given her while on deployment, which had a profound effect given her location. "There are so many mentions of wars and battles. They're such a recurrent theme from biblical times. And there I was, in the Middle East, not very far from where many of those events took place. There's such history in that region." The reality of the reason for being there had an effect too.

"What made me sad was how much of that area was being destroyed. And humans have been doing that there for what seems like forever. And I was reminded that favor is often given to those who have trusted in God, and who sought to fight for just causes. And, at the time, I believed that we were there fighting for a just cause. And now, being removed from military life for as long as I have, more than ten years, I definitely look differently at the situation."

She had questions about her faith too, struggling with why good people were dying and how God could let it happen. "I did question my faith back then. I had another friend who was killed in Afghanistan just a few weeks before he was scheduled to come home. And there are those others I mentioned, and then even after I was home for good, I had military friends die from injuries or suicide. So now, even more than then, I've had a lot of internal struggles and questions of why and what was it all for."

But her faith continues to grow over time. And as it does, "those struggles get easier," she said. "When you're in the thick of it, and you are losing people that are close to you, it is easy to be angry because that doesn't make sense, absolutely no sense."

Like so many other combat veterans, faith gives Jessica a greater perspective on it all, and serves as a source for peace. "But then, on the other hand, it's a great gift to have had those experiences. It's a gift if you choose to look at it that way. That's true because, one, I knew some of these people so well, so deeply, and they were the most amazing humans. And having those losses makes you look at life totally different. You definitely realize how precious and valuable our lives are. You see things through a different lens. You see clearly that we have a different purpose here. And those really big questions change a bit. It isn't just why did that happen. It's a different why: Why are we here? What are we on this earth to do?"

Her initial *why* questions haven't gone away completely, and she doesn't expect they ever will. "I still battle with them. And I might not fully understand those whys in this lifetime. Those answers may not come until later. But through faith in God, I know that I'm going to be reunited with those friends again. I'll see God. I'll see them. We'll all be Home."

*   *   *

That is the fulfillment of the promise that God makes to us all, and the peace that comes with the assurance that we will be together with those we loved and lost once again in heaven. Jessica's skills as a combat medic are matched only by her compassion for her loved ones, her commitment to keeping alive the souls under her care, and, first and foremost, the faith she crystallized when she needed God most.

God prepared Jessica her entire life to be there at the exact right moment, with the exact right skills and courage, when those warriors were injured. God heard her prayers the night she deployed, and He was with her as she tended to those wounded in war, an angel in a helmet on the battlefield reassuring her fellow soldiers, "I've got this."

For He shall give His angels charge over you,
to keep you in all your ways. In their hands they shall bear you up, Lest
you dash your foot against a stone.

PSALM 91:11–12

7/24/45-JOE'S GRAVE

My great-great aunt Lieutenant Luella
Lorenz, who was able to visit her little
brother's grave twice during her WWII
deployment as a US Army nurse.

My great-great grandmother Rosa Lorenz, after whom I am named,
at the grave of her son in Suresnes in 1930, part of the
Gold Star Mothers Pilgrimage.

Chaplain Doug Collins, a dedicated Air Force colonel and former US Representative for Georgia's Ninth Congressional District, exemplifies a lifelong commitment to service.

7

Ministering to the Minister

Chaplain, Colonel
Doug Collins,
US Air Force

Chaplain Doug Collins has the ultimate servant's heart. A current colonel and chaplain in the United States Air Force, he is also a former congressman who represented Georgia's Ninth District and the pastor of a church. Chaplain Collins is an ebullient family man, a loyal friend, a deeply kind individual, and an authentic representative of the people. He's also a combat veteran.

There are multiple roles in the theater of war, multiple vital parts soldiers play. It is the chaplains who stand by, serving the soldiers' spiritual needs, supporting the warriors who bear the unimaginable burden of combat. The pressures and stressors of war take a heavy toll; warriors depend on chaplains to help guide them through pain and loss, physical injury, and moral injury. Moreover, those deployed are often managing multiple challenges on the home front on top of the complexities of war. And families of the fallen and injured lean on these chaplains in times of unimaginable sorrow and questioning too.

These special souls serve many capacities beyond leading Sunday services—it is they who absorb the pain and anguish, the questions and fear held by so many. It is these chaplains who steadfastly support those who are falling. But who ministers to them?

A Military Chaplain's Calling

"The chaplain's main job is to provide for the religious liberties of—and freedom of expression for—those who serve," Chaplain Doug Collins explained. "And that means anybody. A chaplain is there for a person of no faith, someone who is adversarial, and also those who have the same faith as that chaplain or have a different faith. Sometimes that concept is misunderstood." Chaplain Collins is a Southern Baptist, but he's there for everyone; his role is God-called.

Chaplain Collins has led a life of service to his faith and to his country, and is a shining light among many. He typifies the spirit of giving that infuses the fabric of our identity as Americans. After graduating from North Georgia College and State University in 1998 with a degree in political science and criminal law, he chose to join the Navy and serve as a chaplain there. It meant giving up the opportunity to serve in the Judge Advocate General's (JAG) Corps as an attorney.

He decided, for a time, to sacrifice his post-Navy legal career to serve God in another way. After the September 11, 2001, terrorist attacks, he heard God's call. He volunteered to join the United States Air Force Reserve Command. Once again, he opted to work as a chaplain, this time out of the 94th Airlift Wing at Dobbins Air Reserve Base in Marietta, Georgia. During the Iraq war, he went downrange to Balad Air Base in 2008.

Along with his military service, his law practice, and other civilian jobs, in 2007 Chaplain Collins was elected to the Georgia House of Representatives, where he served two terms from 2007 to 2013. In November 2012, Georgia's voters then elected him to represent its Ninth District in the US House. In Congress he proudly served Georgians from 2013 to 2021. He also was shepherd of a flock, pastoring at Chicopee Baptist Church. He and his wife, Linda, have three children.

The Chaplain in War

In combat, people are highly sensitive to issues of life and death. Soldiers are coming face-to-face with those realities in a combat zone, and lean heavily on their chaplains. "God has given us a wonderful mosaic of moments, not hours or days, but moments," Chaplain Collins said. "And the soldiers have an openness that you do not see in most places."

"That's all I can do," he added. "If any chaplain, any pastor, no matter where they are in the world, believes it is their job to do everything, well, they're going to be burned-out very quickly. My job was not to be the start, finish, and the save. My job is only to lay out an opportunity." Then God does the rest.

In 2008, Chaplain Collins was stationed at Balad Air Base, the site of the Air Force control base. Balad is just north of Baghdad, in the so-called Sunni Triangle area, not far from Saddam Hussein's hometown of Tikrit. A large complex, it was located in the center of much of the action at that time, with between 30,000 and 40,000 personnel going in and out of it.

Just weeks into the 2003 invasion, Baghdad fell, but by the time Chaplain Collins was in-country, the Sunni minority and the Shia majority in the triangular territory formed by those three cities were still engaged in violent resistance to the US-led occupation. With Saddam Hussein hailing from that area, loyalties to him and his regime ran deep. So did the Sunnis' fear that their thirty years of dominance were at an end. The Old Testament is filled with stories of tribes in battle for control and domination. That tale continues throughout the world today, and most fiercely in the Middle East. Our troops had their work cut out for them, but they could count on the blessing of spiritual guidance and support that men like Chaplain Collins provided.

The Brotherhood

Chaplain Collins spent much of his time at the medical facility at Balad, renowned for the caliber of its combat medical staff. "I wish that I could say that all those wounded made it. Some did not make it, even when they arrived at state-of-[the]-art military hospitals overseas and back home. I'll never forget one young Army soldier who was wounded during an attack. He was brought in earlier in the day before I was there. He was on one of the beds, and he was pretty beat up. They'd been working on him the whole time. Some of his other platoon mates and others were in the same hospital but weren't hurt as bad."

Chaplain Collins frequently went to visit patients at the hospital. He would form connections with them, learning more about the soldier and what had happened. But with these particular young men the conversation was different. "The only thing they wanted to talk about was that gravely wounded soldier." Their friend.

The soldier was around the corner from the rest of them. He may have been out of his platoon mates' line of vision, but he wasn't out of their hearts or minds. And he has never left Chaplain Collins's thoughts or prayers either.

"The staff had done everything they could to stabilize him," Chaplain Collins remembered. "I prayed over him; he was not communicative. I talked to the doctors, prayed with the nurses. We saw this kind of thing, unfortunately, every day, but it doesn't take off the sting. He was just a handsome young man, blond and blue eyed, and he reminded me of kids that I knew back at my church, and my son."

The young man made it home to the States, where he passed away. Chaplain Collins learned this devastating update from the *Military Times/Stars and Stripes* newspaper. "At the bottom of page four or five, they would have a section about those who had died in the previous week or two in the war zones. I opened it up a week or so after that young man was brought in."

Then Chaplain Collins stopped cold. He realized he had had direct contact with four of the nine soldiers who had died. "I've got that paper still to this day. I kept it as a reminder."

His experience is a reminder of the complex emotions in war, the raw pain, the bond those warriors share. "But it also showed the helplessness you can feel at times," Chaplain Collins said. "You can feel what the doctors are feeling after all they had done. But you take solace in what we and the doctors had done there. They got this individual home. My understanding was that he would have probably had a chance to have family members close by when he passed."

Perhaps the greatest gift for a soldier who makes the Ultimate Sacrifice was the chance to be with loved ones before being called Home. Chaplain Collins was part of the incredible teams who endeavored to ensure that could happen.

Ministering in the Gap

Chaplain Collins served one night a week as the nighttime flight-line chaplain. His ministry often involved fielding big questions. "I would find that most of the time God would open the door through a question, not necessarily one that I asked," he reflected. "More than a few times someone would ask 'How could this happen?' Or how could something difficult going on back home be happening?"

One such young soldier had just arrived on station at Balad. "And I'll never understand this, but his wife calls him that first day to tell him that she wants a divorce."

Chaplain Collins shook his head. "And I get involved because he's not effective in his job. He's suicidal.

"And that's the other thing that chaplains are asked to do—to make sure that these men and women can be effective and do their job. We're there to give those young people—most of them are young—the freedom, an outlet, to discuss problems, to discuss fears, discuss life, and to provide answers for them at a time and a place in their lives where answers may not be found. And faith plays a huge role in answering those questions and help them to do the job they're paid to do."

God is everywhere and can be found anywhere. You don't have to be inside the brick and mortar of a church, or within the structure of a church service, to feel Him. And often, the most transformative ministry occurs in real time, in the gap, in those moments when people least expect it, but need it the most.

The Minister to the Minister

As military chaplains minister to so many in need, they absorb much of the heartbreak themselves. Chaplain Collins witnessed firsthand the toll war can take on those who were there to counsel and guide those on the front lines.

"Still to this day, one of the worst cases of post-traumatic stress (PTS) I've seen was with a fellow chaplain, a pastor," Chaplain Collins shared. "Downrange, your life gets turned upside down and inside out. Your daily pattern is all screwed up, up at night going out on operations. I was alone after having gone out with the boys on their operation, and went to get 'lunch' at about one or two in the morning. I sat at a table doing some reading, getting ready for a Bible study session I had coming up. Where we ate was a huge warehouse-type building that could hold thousands, and it was just one of three on base. That time of night it was nearly empty, some of the night-shift folks in there having a meal.

"I was busy eating and working, and I looked up and saw this man at another table over a few from mine," Chaplain Collins described. "He was seated alone also. He had an Army T-shirt on, his PT gear. We nodded hello like people do, and I got back to reading. Next thing I knew, he was walking toward me. He sat down, and he seemed very happy—maybe too happy. I knew something wasn't right. I sensed that he was fake-euphoric. We greeted one another and he went on to tell me that he was a chaplain, a part of the Army garrison."

As the men began to talk about different things, it became clear that the man had adopted a fake *Hey, everything's fine—I'm fine* demeanor. "I could see that he had on this brave face that he thought he needed to put on for everybody else to see," Chaplain Collins said. "But the more we talked, I could see behind that brave face. And the more it was clear that he was broken and that he missed his family, that he was questioning everything about why he was there." It got worse. "The longer we talked, the more he shared about his family and issues back home with them. I was watching this man deteriorate before my eyes. Then he said he was eight months into a twelve-month deployment."

At that point in 2008, many of our service personnel were away from home for a year at a time. Often, they'd come home only to be redeployed quickly. With only about 1 percent of our total population serving in Iraq and Afghanistan, the quick turnaround times were considered a necessity, but it took its toll on those who maintained that grueling schedule.

That included chaplains who were subject to the same rotations. Chaplain Collins has sounded the alarm about PTS and the catastrophic impact of multiple deployments this generation of warriors has endured. In this particular case, that chaplain had been away from family about 80 percent of the time since the war began in 2003.

"He had gotten to the point where pastoring and being a chaplain every day had become a kind of twisted game. He told me it was get-through-the-day, get-through-the-day every day. He wanted—and needed—to go home," Chaplain Collins said. "Toward the end of our conversation, that became really clear. He'd told his command that he didn't want to be there. In the past, he'd said that he didn't want to go downrange again, but he was sent anyway.

"He was not in good shape by the end of that hour-and-a-half conversation we had there in the DFAC, the dining facility. He went from the façade of a chaplain to the brokenness of a real, honest human being who admitted several times that he simply didn't know what to do." That's when Chaplain Collins became truly alarmed.

He felt the man was settled enough that he could now take him back to his housing unit. He knew there would be others there who could keep vigil over him. Chaplain Collins was duty-bound to report what he had witnessed, and he had that chaplain's blessing to advocate for him going home. Chaplain Collins even went up the chain of command, because it was obvious this chaplain was no longer capable of being effective.

His heart went out to this man. Eventually, Chaplain Collins learned the chaplain had been sent home. That experience, that conversation, offered Chaplain Collins more insight into the role chaplains play, and the lengths they go through to ensure everyone around them is taken care of. It risks no one seeing them hurting too.

"The world doesn't need to see your façade," he said. "They need to see who you *really* are. And chaplains and caregivers may be the worst offenders. We try to make everybody else better. And we're like the plumber whose house has the worst plumbing issues. A cobbler who has holes in his shoes. Except our problem is we're trying to lead people to the Almighty, and we get in a bad way sometimes because we don't understand all things all the time. And I take great faith in knowing that in scripture, I'm in pretty good company. There were a lot of people who—even in the presence of Jesus—questioned. *And that's okay*. I'm open with people about my questions and struggles."

As a colonel now, Chaplain Collins has taken on a more leadership role, and he encourages members of the chaplaincy to minister to each other. "There's this idea in the military and in law enforcement—and my father was in law enforcement for thirty years—that asking for help, saying you are scared, is a sign of weakness," he said. "And chaplains and ministers have to do a lot of pouring out. But you can only pour out what's been poured into you. And when you're empty, then you're really struggling. It's easy to become like that chaplain I spoke with that time in the DFAC in Balad. He was an empty vessel."

The realities of war for our troops can destroy even the strongest men and women: unendurable separation from loved ones; losing brothers in arms; fighting in intense battles; constantly under threat; managing home front stressors and difficulties from so far away. The importance of the chaplain's role to guide, support, and help care for the spiritual and emotional welfare of these warriors cannot be overstated—but sometimes even chaplains need a break. Only the Living Water keeps us truly satiated, and vessels need refilling.

Filling the Vessel

Sometimes in the chaos of war, it is the members of the flock that minister to the chaplain. Chaplain Collins had a sweet experience at the Balad gate that ended up being a God-moment for him. One night as he was waiting at the gate to reenter the complex, no one came out. He waited. Still no one came out. Chaplain Collins joked to himself, "Well, did they all go back home to the States and no one told me?"

Finally, a young man came hustling out, carrying his weapon and apologizing profusely for making Chaplain Collins wait. He had been in the back doing something else. Chaplain Collins knew him by name and reassured him it was no problem, then told him he was glad that the young man hadn't made his colonel or his captain wait!

"'Yes, sir,' he told me. 'I agree with that.'" Chaplain Collins smiled at the recollection of the airman 1C recognizing his good fortune. "One thing about being a chaplain is that you can tell a guy to get his stuff straight without actually having to discipline him. So I talked to him a bit longer, and came to find out that he was back in the guard shack working on a budget. This was back in 2008, and we were still in the housing crisis. His dad was now out of work as a tradesman, and things were tough financially back home. That was why this A1C had joined the military."

The airman told Chaplain Collins that now that he was making big money, he needed to do this budget so that he could figure out how much he could keep and how much he could send home. The chaplain had to laugh. "The airman was nineteen or twenty years old, and to him, that pay he was getting was 'big money.'"

Then Chaplain Collins grew contemplative. "But really, it showed what a big heart he had. He wanted to send money home so that his sister could get a computer for school. He wanted to send money home for things his younger brothers wanted. And I thought about this and wondered what it would be like if more of us back home in the US could prioritize living better and helping each other out."

Chaplain Collins saw this as his own God-moment. "Not every chaplain moment involves running in to save the day. This was a story of me riding up to the gate, having to wait, and then driving off past the gate with tears in my eyes and thanking God for showing me what He just did. God poured that in me, His vessel, so that I could pour it out later in service to others."

This seemingly small interaction had a deep impact, which in turn impacted countless others through the Chaplain's dedicated ministry. By filling his own vessel with significant moments connecting with others, regardless of rank, regardless of expectation, Chaplain Collins was primed to continue humbly serving others.

The Safest Place

Chaplain Collins often ministered to those who asked those "why" questions that troubled both mind and soul. Within the Air Force, advances in technology made some aspects of warfare safer but also exposed personnel to a new and different potential cause of moral injury. "In Iraq and Afghanistan at that time, the known use of drones began. Those advanced weapons were operated remotely. Their pilots were often thousands of miles away from wherever they were being launched. Those drone pilots were back here in the United States, seated in air-conditioned rooms, controlling those drones that were delivering deadly payloads.

"Sometimes they could press a button, get up from their console, end their day, and drive home to their neighborhood where everybody's happy," Chaplain Collins explained. "They may take their kids to ball practice and everything is normal and nice. We started to see those performing those drone tasks having the same moral questions arise as ground forces who were involved in door-to-door combat. They'd get an order and they'd execute it, taking out bad guys, but there was always the question of collateral damage—killing or injuring others who just happened to be in the wrong place at the wrong time."

They might have been safer physically, but this particular situation presented particular challenges to their mental health. "While they're back at home and their spouse is cooking dinner, they couldn't talk about what their day was like at work. You can't share that."

Chaplains have a unique role to play in dealing with moral injury. "Our abilities as a chaplain are particularly suited to what I was seeing happening to some pilots and drone pilots. Someone coming to see us knows that they enjoy one hundred percent confidentiality. They own the conversation. I am, as an Air Force chaplain, the safe place that you can come to.

"I'm not there to analyze," Chaplain Collins said. "I'm there to help. I'm there to provide a faith perspective that you're not alone. You are not doing this by yourself. You are *not*. There's a reason that you are a created being. God breathed life into you and He would not abandon you. That's a unique role that transcends the moment. It transcends this life. A chaplain must be able to guide people for the life that you live here and give you hope of a life that is yet to come."

* * *

All the afflictions of normal life affect deployed soldiers too, with the added turmoil of war. Our warriors face injuries and death and fighting and stress in combat, while managing home finances, new children, marital stressors, ailing loved ones, professional angst, and family separation. In this age of technology, sometimes the presence of moral injury can occur just a short commute from home.

The kaleidoscope of needs requires a Swiss Army knife kind of chaplain; one who has the compassion and heart to identify what these soldiers need, even if sometimes it's just a friendly connection, the offer of a truly safe place to lament. Chaplain Collins sees the Jesus in all of these earnest troops; the vessels who need filling, the hearts who need comfort, the minds who need help answering big questions. And ultimately, to ensure that his fellow chaplains aren't left behind in their quest to buoy others. These stories reflect the complexities of serving as a military chaplain and the realities they face. They are human too. And Chaplain Collins is a very special one. A force multiplier with a servant's heart.

So Christ himself gave the apostles, the prophets, the evangelists,

the pastors and teachers, to equip his people for works of service, so that

the body of Christ may be built up until we all reach unity in the faith

and in the knowledge of the Son of God and become mature, attaining

to the whole measure of the fullness of Christ.

—EPHESIANS 4:11–13

US troops securing an airfield in Baido, Somalia,
to ensure that relief supplies are secure.

PART II

World War II, Korea, and Vietnam

Colonel Tom Moe returning to US soil as
part of Operation Homecoming.

The Nimitz Carrier Strike Group and embarked CVW-11 en route to
San Diego, California, following an eight-month deployment to the
Arabian Gulf in support of Operation Iraqi Freedom.

Captain Charlie Plumb outside the cockpit
of his F-4 Phantom jet.

8

Keep the Faith, Baby!

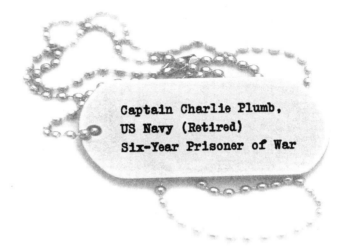

```
Captain Charlie Plumb,
US Navy (Retired)
Six-Year Prisoner of War
```

Captain Charlie "Plumber" Plumb was—and remains—the best of the best. A Naval Academy alumnus and graduate of the Navy Fighter Weapons School (what is now known as "Top Gun"), Charlie was living the American Dream. From his origins on a farm in rural Kansas to the cockpit of the US Navy's hottest fighter jet, the F-4 Phantom, Charlie was seemingly unstoppable. It was May 1967 and America was in the thick of the Vietnam War. Charlie had flown seventy-four successful combat missions over North Vietnam and made over one hundred aircraft carrier landings.

Then on his seventy-fifth mission—just five days before the end of his tour—Charlie was shot down over Hanoi. He was taken prisoner of war (POW), and spent the next 2,103 days in brutally torturous captivity.

Yet those days were also spent in secret worship, forging unbreakable fellowship, with Christ dwelling among them. This is the story of spiritual freedom despite physical prison.

Rich in Love, Strong in Faith

Charlie was born during World War II, and when his father was drafted, their family moved to a tiny town in Kansas. There Charlie began his spiritual journey at the Evangelical United Brethren Church. Around the time that he was becoming a teen, he accepted Christ as his Savior while attending a church camp in Salinas, Kansas.

The economic prosperity that the war effort produced had not reached rural Kansas. Charlie joked that his family was very rich: they had an indoor toilet by the time he was seven. He added, "We were rich in unity and love, and I loved that little church. We gathered every Sunday morning and every Wednesday evening and praised God."

When he arrived as a young plebe at the United States Naval Academy in Annapolis, Maryland, he swore the oath to defend the country against all enemies, foreign and domestic. Charlie recalled not being sure what he was committing himself to. But in this new environment, he found something familiar to anchor him. He attended mandatory chapel services each Sunday and became involved in the Officers' Christian Union throughout his time at Annapolis. Although he didn't know it at the time, this helped prepare him later to serve his fellow POWs spiritually in Vietnam.

As Charlie put it, "We thumped our Bibles in the basement of Bancroft Hall and learned the basic tenets of putting together a religious service aboard a ship."

Before he left for Vietnam, he said goodbye to his wife and told her that he would be back in eight months. He nearly made good on that pledge.

Seventy-four successful combat missions under his wing, he was five days from going home when his F-4 Phantom jet was hit by a surface-to-air missile.

Captured

Charlie and his radar intercept officer (RIO) both ejected. They had survived the explosion but were hardly safe. "The opening shock of the parachute was a pretty physically dramatic endeavor," Charlie recalled. "I was right near the city of Hanoi. Peasant farmers were on the ground with their rifles, shooting at me. I thought that was not necessary," he said, chuckling with remarkable aplomb. "They just knocked my airplane out of the sky, and now they're shooting at the pilot!"

He prayed for his wife. "I had left her on her birthday, as a matter of fact, and didn't really prepare her for having a prisoner of war as a husband. Somebody that she couldn't talk to, communicate with, even to let her know I was alive. I thought back to that moment in time when I'm handling the parachute. I said to myself, 'Dummy. Why didn't you make a deal with God and promise to be righteous and sober, a godly guy the rest of your life? Tell Him you'll go to church every Sunday morning.' Just 'Lord, send me a little wind to push me back to the ocean where the good guys could rescue me.' I didn't need much wind; ten to twelve knots, gusting to forty. But I'd take whatever He had to offer."

Half reflective and half dodging bullets while he parachuted down, Charlie's sense of humor and bright spirit shone through as he described that dramatic, and piercingly poignant, scene. Then it became simply terrifying.

"I wound up about waist-deep in a rice paddy," Charlie continued. "It was like a scene from a Frankenstein movie when the townspeople confront him while he's loose in their village. They carried farm tools—machetes, shovels, rakes, and hoes. I was outnumbered and I'd seen that my RIO had landed about a half mile away. We'd both survived and so that was a good thing. I surrendered."

Charlie endured a very rough capture and was taken to a prison constructed by the French to house Vietnamese prisoners. The cells were eight feet by eight feet, with low ceilings. Because Vietnamese men were generally much smaller than the typical American, they wouldn't have been as oppressed by the small size of the cells as Charlie and the other POWs were. The "tools" of the prison were also too small. Decades later, Charlie's wrists still bear the scars from the gaping wounds under the ever-present manacles that severely gouged his flesh.

What Charlie endured even on that first day was enough to break any man. Yet far more challenging were the torture sessions that hallmarked his years in captivity. Charlie had an advantage, however, that his captors couldn't overcome. His faith was stronger than any physical torture. And his prayers kept him connected to God.

"I was having a type of out-of-body experience, hoping that would ameliorate the pain," he recalled of one such session. "But I felt comfort in my faith, even from the very beginning. I knew for sure there was a plan, that God was in control of this. And that I may never know the reason why I'm going through this. But I prayed that there might be some value in the pain. And I was quite certain there would be, though I also knew that I might never figure out what that value would be."

The enemy tried to tear down Charlie's faith, but never came close to succeeding. "They always wanted us to deny our religion," Charlie said. "I had an interrogator, six months into my ordeal, who said to me, 'Why do you continue to call on your God? Don't you realize your God has forsaken you? How could a loving God put you in this situation?' He'd argue this point with me, but their being deniers didn't have the effect they wanted. It only strengthened my convictions."

A Prison Worse Than Prison

Regardless of Charlie's strength in God and faith, the physical torture was simply unbearable. He was held in solitary confinement and subject to regular gruesome torture sessions. The Uniform Code of Military Justice governed what POWs like Charlie were and were not obligated to do and say while in captivity. Charlie was only to state his name, rank, and serial number to the enemy. Initially, Charlie was sure he could and would adhere to the code. Torture overwhelmed him. When he broke, he was subsequently racked with guilt. Along with four serious open physical wounds, Charlie struggled with his perception that he was weak.

"It got to the point that I didn't want to go home after the war," Charlie remembered. "I thought I'd go to some other country and change my name. I didn't want anyone to know how I'd failed to honor that commitment. I felt very, very dejected and very, very alone and very, very guilty."

My heart ached for this honorable man with incredible character, who had endured the unendurable with faith and sheer will. The thought he could possibly view himself as anything less than strong, worthy, valuable, and approved by his fellow countrymen and before God felt incomprehensible. There are different kinds of prisons in war, and not all are made of brick and mortar.

Then, one day, everything changed. "I was in my cell and I heard a cricket. I walked over to take a look in the corner, expecting to find that insect. Instead, I saw a small wire coming through a rat hole at the base of the cell wall. I had to consider the possibilities. I didn't think it was the enemy. The enemy wasn't sophisticated enough to try to trick me with the wire. And if it wasn't the enemy, then it was somebody trying to communicate with me."

Someone Cares

Charlie was torn. He knew it was likely that dozens and dozens of other fighter pilots had been taken prisoner too. He would have loved to communicate with someone, but he was still overcome by guilt. Charlie sat for an hour thinking. All that time, the wire moved in the rat hole, making that cricket sound. He was also worried the guards could hear it. Whoever was on the other side of that wall could get in trouble—big trouble. He made a decision. He tugged at the wire.

That first tug was the first step in Charlie learning an extensive code of communication that the American POWs had developed. Being in solitary confinement was torturous in and of itself. Neuroscientists have revealed that the impact of isolation has the same negative physical effect on the brain as physical pain does. Making contact with another human being—one who wasn't bent on inflicting pain on you—was truly inspiriting. "Even if the communication system was slow, archaic, and cumbersome, it was a lifesaver," Charlie told me.

Although counterintuitive to say so, Charlie was fortunate he was "only" in solitary confinement for four months. He learned that others had been in that mentally, spiritually, and physically horrific sustained state for four and a half years. To exist in total darkness was overwhelmingly disorienting, and at times he wondered whether he was really alive.

"The simple tugging on the wire back let me know that I *was* alive. Someone was responding to me. Second, it told me that someone cared about me."

Charlie later found out that it was Lieutenant Commander Robert "Bob" Shumaker at the other end of that wire. Bob was another fighter pilot and had already been selected by NASA to become an astronaut. Bob's role while in captivity was to get the new prisoners into the fold as quickly as possible. The seasoned POWs understood it was so crucial that Charlie and others like him didn't linger too long in the literal and figurative dark place. Their lives depended on it. Against all odds, Bob fenagled the wire to Charlie even though their two cells were separated by an entire storage closet. Bob also made a quick diagnosis based on his own experience.

"Bob said that I was suffering from a disease," Charlie recalled. "He didn't know the real name for it, but said they referred to it as 'prison disease.' He eventually told me that the symptoms were blaming everybody else for your problems, feeling sorry for yourself,

121

and assuming you have no control over your destiny." The attitude was fundamental—because the stakes were life and death.

Bob told Charlie there was a cure: keeping the faith. Through the painstaking communication of wire tugs, Bob told Charlie that bottom line, the guys who survived this prison ordeal believed in things—not just faith in God, but faith in yourself, faith in country, and faith in your flag. They lived, Bob told Charlie, according to this motto: *Keep the faith, baby!*

Charlie kept learning. When Charlie questioned the need for a hierarchy of leadership among the POWs when they were confined to an eight-by-eight-foot cell, he was told that they were more concerned with the eight inches between the men's ears. There were lessons about behavior too, fundamental shift changes that equipped the men with the best survival and endurance odds possible. Charlie learned they were to resist their captors at every opportunity, from the most minor to the most major.

The first of those was never to make a ceremonial bow to their enemy. Soon word spread throughout the entire prison camp that this was the order they had to follow. When Charlie was transferred to another camp, he brought with him both the code to communicate and the code of conduct they used to defy their captors.

We Mattered

The Americans and loved ones on the home front played a role in their survival too. POW wives petitioned the US government to keep pressure on the North Vietnamese to end the use of torture. Working with the wives of three missing pilots, a Los Angeles–based student organization called Voices in Vital America (VIVA), co-chaired by Bob Hope and Martha Raye in addition to the student founder, produced commemorative bracelets engraved with the name, rank, and date of loss of Americans held as POWs or those missing in action (MIA). Nickel-plated bracelets were sold to students for $2.50, the price of a student admission to the local movie theater, and copper-plated bracelets were sold to adults for $3.00; the buyer pledged to wear it until the individual or his or her remains were returned to the US, after which the wearer would return the bracelet to the family or person whose name was engraved in the metal. In all, VIVA distributed nearly five million bracelets and raised enough money to produce untold millions of bumper stickers, buttons, newspaper ads, and so on to draw attention to the missing and captive Americans.

Wed. May 31st

Dearest Barbara —

Ever since we had the news about Charlie, I've been trying to form a letter to you but not knowing how to do so. As parents, we are heart-broken, of course — as his wife, it must be even worse. God is our only refuge — we must trust Him to bring Charles back to us, although I'm sure he all ready — it may be quite a while before this comes to pass.

It is hard to understand why this had to happen to Charles. I'm trying so hard not to be selfish in my prayers but it isn't easy. Charles has so much to give, to offer — it's hard to understand why he must be put in a position where he can do nothing. But who knows, maybe this is a plan by which he can even do greater things.

Barbara, forgive me — I know I'm not making much sense but this is

Charlie's mother, Marjorie, writing to his wife, Barbara, to express her anguish and faith upon learning that Charlie had been shot down.

Charlie also saw they served another purpose. Perhaps the most important function of all.

"They were going to pray for me. I didn't know their names, but they knew mine. This commemoration meant that we *mattered*."

It had a very real effect. "Our enemy started to treat us better. And, for the most part, they stopped torturing us."

By Charlie's fourth year as a prisoner of war, conditions and treatment were improving. But the Americans still maintained a strict, cohesive code of conduct that sent the message they would never capitulate to enemy demands or desires. The North Vietnamese began to release prisoners. The American POWs agreed unanimously that they would accept release only in the order of capture.

Among those initially selected to return home by the North Vietnamese was Charlie's fellow Annapolis alumni and former flight instructor, then–Lieutenant Commander John McCain. John's father was an admiral in the US Navy and the enemy recognized the propaganda value of releasing him first. But McCain refused the out-of-sequence repatriation unless every man taken before him was also released. This refusal led to increased torture sessions, regular beatings, and additional solitary confinement for McCain. The defiance and strength, the brotherhood, and honor exhibited by McCain and the American POWs against the enemy was nothing short of legendary. They will forever remain among our nation's absolute best and bravest.

In Prison, Yet Free

Charlie was later returned to the Hanoi, North Vietnam, prisoner complex, known among the POWs as the "Hanoi Hilton." The men were housed in a twenty-by-thirty-foot room with fourteen inches of bed space. Charlie was in a room with fifty-six other prisoners. They had gone from one extreme to the other, but as Charlie said, "The living conditions were terrible. But it was also wonderful. We were finally there together. We were finally able to see one another. We could talk to each other, tell stories, and play games."

There was one more added benefit. A blessing at the real heart of Charlie's experience as a POW.

In communist North Vietnam, religion was forbidden, but the men defied that stricture. Because of Charlie's chaplain training at the Naval Academy, POW leadership asked him to start their own small church and serve as their chaplain.

The men fashioned a small cross and altar out of clothes, which they could quickly hide away. They couldn't be seen kneeling or singing hymns. To avoid detection and punishment, the Americans needed a guard; three men volunteered. The men worked out a system to alert Charlie to a guard's approach.

Captain Charlie Plumb's Silver Star Citation

For conspicuous gallantry and intrepidity while interned as a Prisoner of War in North Vietnam. In September 1967, his captors, completely ignoring international agreements, subjected him to extreme mental and physical cruelties in an attempt to obtain military information and false confessions for propaganda purposes. Through his resistance to those brutalities, he contributed significantly toward the eventual abandonment of harsh treatment by the North Vietnamese, which was attracting international attention. By his determination, courage, resourcefulness, and devotion to duty, he reflected great credit upon himself and upheld the highest traditions of the Naval Service and the United States Armed Forces.

The men went on a hunger strike to force the prison officials to give them a Bible. It didn't work right away. The highest-ranking man in their prisoner community was Jewish, and he encouraged the men to press on with the strike. Finally, the enemy relented.

"It was a miracle that guys devised a way to get us water during the hunger strike," Charlie said. "It was another miracle that we got our dirty, old, ragged copy of the Bible. What I found interesting is that I was the one in charge of the Bible, and I can't tell you the number of guys who came up to me and just wanted to touch the Holy Scripture.

"The three POW guards were avowed atheists. They were among the first in line to touch it. That meant they had faith, but they just couldn't verbalize it. In the end, though, the guards took the Bible away after a day and a half. Some guys acted as scribes and copied portions of it on toilet paper using a quill pen made from a stick of bamboo."

The spectacular resolve, the creative ingenuity, the dedication to worship these men displayed while they were prisoners of war. They went without food for the chance to have God's Word. Then to have a Bible for a mere day and a half, but to serve in that time as witness to the power within; the simple touch by these spiritual giants of the utter freedom and salvation the Holy Book represents had a greater impact on those men than words can ever express. And God was in their midst, as they gathered in His name. The Word via a bamboo quill pen. A cross of two sticks. An altar of rags. These men were physically in prison but spiritually free.

The Magic of Christmas Endures

The men celebrated the birth of our Savior every Christmas, in special, meaningful, and all-too-fleeting ways. And not without punishment. For each of his last three Christmases spent in captivity, Charlie was housed along with Lieutenant Commander Danny Glenn, a fighter pilot and talented artist who had studied architecture at the University of Oklahoma. Each year, Charlie asked Danny to produce a piece of art depicting a Christmas scene. The first was a Nativity scene.

"Danny walked all around the camp and found bits of brick—you can't imagine how many different shades he could find—and scratched those chunks down to make a powder to later make into a paint," Charlie described. "That Nativity scene was on a wall, and we kept it covered with rags."

"It was the most beautiful Nativity scene I'd ever had my eyes on," Charlie remembered. "There were the Wise Men, the angels, the baby Jesus in the manger. But before we could have our Christmas Eve mass, in walked the enemy guards. They scrubbed the Nativity scene off the wall and sent us outside in the nude."

The next year Charlie asked Danny if he could paint a large-scale Christmas tree. Danny depicted a tree with a star on top, strung popped corn, lights, and ornaments. All of it was a mosaic of dyed toilet paper. Once again the guards came in. Down went the Christmas mosaic. Off went the men's clothes. Out they went into the courtyard.

The third time around, just before Christmas found Danny and Charlie in their darkened cell, planning and plotting. This time, however, Danny needed Charlie to convince him. He was exhausted by the immediate destruction by the enemy and the severe resulting punishment they had to endure.

Finally, Danny came around. He asked Charlie what art he wanted for Christmas.

"I told him that it was really dark in that cell. I wanted a slide show. I wanted some light to celebrate that season."

To stay ahead of the guards, the men planned to celebrate Christmas early, on December 22. The men had been issued cigarettes and matches, and Charlie managed to fashion a candle out of them. Using toilet paper and rice glue, they formed figures—the Wise Men, crèche, the shepherds, and the baby Jesus. Holding those small statues in front of the candlelit tube, they projected shadow scenes on the walls of their prison cell. Dan and Charlie spent that early Christmas in captivity singing carols and hymns, basking in the glow of the scene of our Savior's birth, of Christ our Lord.

The magic of Christmas lies in its heart: "For God so loved the world, He gave His one and only Son, that whoever believes in Him should not perish but have eternal life" (John 3:16). "And the Word became flesh and dwelt among us, and we have seen His glory, glory of the only Son from the Father, full of grace and truth" (John 1:14). These prisoners of war, enduring years of torture and religious persecution in their own confines, pursued the most creative, heartfelt ways to celebrate the birth of Jesus. Distilled down to love, fellowship, and worship, these men experienced Christmas in a pure form, despite enemy attacks and physical punishment. I have no doubt Gabriel and all the angels in heaven were rejoicing alongside these brave warriors of the Army of Christ, who created their own magic in their dark prison cells.

Forgiving and Free

There was one final component to Charlie's survival, and to living freely after he gained his physical freedom back: forgiveness.

Charlie was righteously angry at the beginning of his capture. He shared that with Bob Shumaker via the wire, who delivered this message: "Anger does more harm to the vessel it is stored in than on the subject on which it's poured." Indeed, the fear of man, or anger, will prove to be a snare. "Whoever trusts in the Lord is kept safe" (Proverbs 29:25).

Charlie understood. "My anger isn't hurting anybody; it's hurting *me*. And it's going to kill me if I don't forgive. I have a really tight bond with the guys I was imprisoned

127

with. We each claim that we saved one another's life. And they all went through the same process of anger that I did. Maybe for different reasons, but they went through it."

He paused. "Anger *and* guilt. But we all learned to forgive. My mother was the epitome of forgiveness. Her philosophy on the subject was this: In order to be offended you have to accept that offense. So, in that way, she taught me a lot about forgiveness.

"Today, I can go to Washington, DC, and walk along the Vietnam War memorial wall and not be angry. I see the names of buddies on there and I'm not angry. I don't accept that offense. I have that choice. Knowing I could choose forgiveness over anger and guilt made a tremendous difference in my survival."

*   *   *

Following his repatriation, Charlie continued his Navy flying career in Reserve Squadrons, flying the A-4 Skyhawk, A-7 Corsair, and the F/A-18 Hornet. (Find me another fighter pilot who flew both the Phantom and the Hornet—this is an incredible feat, and a dream of any pilot, let alone most anyone who gazes at the sky in rapture.) He retired from the US Navy after thirty-one years of stellar service. He was awarded the Silver Star, the Legion of Merit, the Bronze Star, two Purple Hearts, Air Medals, a Presidential Unit Citation, and the POW Medal, among other honors.

This remarkable man maintains there are three keys to life and surviving difficult circumstances: attitude is the secret of survival; the power of choice; and no one flies alone. Throughout the almost six years of torturous captivity, Charlie embodied all three. A servant of Christ, a patriot of this nation, and a loyal brother to his fellow POWs, Charlie's steadfast honor is only exceeded by his faith. And maybe his Top Gun pilot skills . . . He is, after all, the best of the best.

But those who wait on the Lord shall renew their strength; they shall mount up with wings like eagles, they shall run and not be weary, they shall walk and not faint.

—ISAIAH 40:31

US soldiers of the 1st Battalion, 9th Cavalry Regiment, approaching
a landing zone in Binh Dinh province in December 1966.

Comedian Bob Hope speaking to
the troops as part of a USO show
at Pearl Harbor in 1944.

The actor Marilyn Monroe
performing for an
appreciative audience in
South Korea as part of a
1954 USO show.

Sergeant Major Darryle Endfinger enjoying a well-deserved
beverage break while serving in Vietnam.

9

One Cup of Coffee with 58,000 Men

Sergeant Major
Darryle Endfinger,
US Army (Retired)

At the height of the Vietnam War, Sergeant Darryle Endfinger was in the thick of the deadliest, largest military offensive campaign. The Rubicon Platoon was steadfast in courage and faith. Suffering ambush after ambush in isolated areas of the Vietnam jungle, Darryle's platoon was seemingly indestructible—until the men suffered a loss that was deemed unfathomable.

Darryle stopped talking to God. The war grew even more intense, the losses even more great. And then one day, amid the most ferocious ambush of them all, God spoke to Darryle. And God saved his life.

Eyes and Ears

Sergeant Major Darryle Endfinger, US Army, was attached to the 101st Airborne Division, serving in Vietnam. He was a member of a reconnaissance platoon. Rubicon Platoon was, as Darryle put it, "the eyes and the ears" of the battalion. He led small groups of men, generally five to seven, who went out at night on foot into the dense jungle and fields on the edge of the A Sâu Valley, near the imperial capital, Hué.

This was in 1968, at the height of the Tet Offensive, one of the largest and deadliest campaigns of the war. The leader of US forces, General William Westmoreland, believed that it would take an additional 200,000 US troops to defeat the Viet Cong and the North Vietnamese People's Army of Vietnam. The US would eventually win, but a war that had become increasingly unpopular among some back home in America became an even more divisive force in America.

The soldiers were insulated to a degree from the unrest at home.

As Darryle pointed out, "You have to remember that back in '67, '68, '69, we didn't even know there was protesting going on back home. We didn't have news media, except for the military publication *Stars and Stripes* and things like that. There was this whole other world we weren't aware of until we got back. We didn't know anything about any negative attitude toward the government. We were soldiers. We were just doing our job. We won our war. We won every major battle in Vietnam. The politicians were the ones who lost the war, not American soldiers. We did what we were supposed to do."

Darryle had always intended on making a career in the service. In various capacities, including being a teacher for ten years in the Junior Reserve Officers' Training Corps (JROTC), he served proudly. He even got to live out his dream of being stationed in Alaska. He found out about getting that assignment during a stopover in Hawaii. From south of the equator to the Great White North, Darryle experienced the full spectrum of Army life during his thirty-three years of service. Through good times and tough times, he remained Army proud.

He served two tours of duty in Vietnam, and when I spoke with him, he pointed to a plaque on the wall behind him. "I don't know if you can see it, but there's twenty-two names on there. And those are the ones from my platoon that died in Vietnam. I carry that plaque with me wherever I go. All the memorials. All the reunions. From 1967 to 1972, we had twenty-two people killed in action."

A Prayerful Soldier

Darryle's faith was strong, but not untested. "I went in as very much a Christian, a young boy, seventeen years old, right out of high school. At home, and even when I reported to Fort Ord and later in training, I knelt down by my bed and prayed. Every time

I was scheduled to make a parachute jump, I went to airborne chapel, and prayed for my safety. And then I prayed again that night for the next day to be safe. Then I looked in the sky after a major battle. So many people were dead. I said, there cannot be a God if He lets things like this happen. Although I knew from all my teachings that these things do happen. But you can lose your faith sometimes. You don't lose your love for God, but understanding why some bad things like that can happen can be very, very hard."

Darryle's faith was eventually restored. But it took time. His mind was consumed in a different way. Fear of failure, of not preparing his own men well and letting them down, preyed on him. Prayer was no longer a part of his life. Darryle's sense of fairness and right and wrong never wavered.

Specialist Donald Green

There was one death from his time in Vietnam that hit him harder than the others —a young man in his unit, Specialist Donald Green. "We went out on a mission together. I was on one side of the hill in my position, and he was on the other. The mortar attack landed on his side and not mine. *Why?* I remember that after advanced infantry training, we went to Fort Benning in Georgia. Then we took a bus to Fort Campbell for our first assignment. Donald was with us.

"I can't forget stopping along the way at a diner and he was refused service because he was black. I grew up in Manteca, California, with six thousand people and only two of them were black. My father never said a prejudicial word in his life. Our platoon spent a year together in Fort Campbell. Of that group, we had four wounded and two killed in Vietnam. That was when I looked up at the sky. Every one of them had a story. One of the guys shouldn't have even been in Vietnam, but there he was.

"A guy named Joe Lopez, our medic, he came over from the other side of the hill. He told me the first person from my recon platoon was dead," Darryle continued. "I asked him who it was, and he told me it was Donald Green. I couldn't believe it. Of all the guys."

"I had to go over three times to where his body lay. He was covered with a poncho, and I just kind of shook his boots, to see if he was really dead. I just could not . . . he was so still. It's hard. He was the first dead American soldier I saw. And he was just so still," Darryle repeated. He was overcome with emotion and so was I.

"I just had to go there and touch his boots, because you hear stories sometimes where they pronounce someone dead, but they're really not. I went over and did that one time.

And I went over two other times, during the evening, and I also said a prayer and offered my respects. Later on, I just lost it. He was the only one of us who was married. He was the only one of us who had a child. *Why him?*"

In the wake of Donald's death, Darryle's struggles with faith grew more difficult. Darryle later found out that even more were killed in action than he knew about at the time. He was quickly learning about the seemingly arbitrary nature of war. The men would form deep bonds, but they could be heartbreakingly brief.

"You'd have coffee in the morning with a guy, then we'd go out on a patrol, and you'd come back and find out through others that somebody had gotten wounded and had to be evacuated. That was it. You never heard any more," Darryle told me. "Now, with technology and social media, you find out that some of those guys later died from their wounds after being put on a helicopter. Things like that really shake you. You just don't know when your time is or who you're going to see at the end of the day. That really shook my faith."

Ambushed and the Unknown

Darryle's job was particularly dangerous. Sent out on scouting missions, he often moved under the cover of darkness and in very small groups. One night during his first deployment, one of his squad mates stopped and pointed. He indicated to Darryle that he had seen something. "Everybody got down inside this cement pagoda," Darryle remembered. "The enemy set up an ambush around our location. They were hoping that we would come in that ambush zone, or one of the other recon patrols would.

"We knew that we had to stay quiet and still and just sit there. I turned off my radio. I didn't want any static or squelch to come out of it and reveal our position. I was supposed to radio back to my platoon leader every hour. I couldn't do that, and so, from ten at night until four in the morning, we were as silent as we could be. At that point, we were able to retrograde out of there—we moved out and slowly made our way around where the enemy was and back to safety at our patrol base. That was a close one."

Shortly afterward, they were moving their entire platoon of twenty to twenty-five soldiers all at once. They were ambushed.

It was horrific. Havoc threatened to disrupt the elite training these warriors had undergone. "The best way I can explain it is that when we got orders, we knew where we were supposed to go and not much else," Darryle said. "We didn't know the results.

Were we going to run into the enemy? Was their element going to be larger than ours? Can we fight them? Do we have enough ammunition to sustain a battle if we do run into a larger enemy force? Do we take the easy way to our position by sticking to established trails? Do we go cross-country? What do we think the enemy thinks we're thinking?"

Darryle was exceedingly observant, as a scout/reconnaissance soldier should be. He wasn't always only on alert for the enemy and taking in the surroundings. He was analyzing the bigger picture, still trying to make sense of it all.

"War for us was streaky. We could go for a few days in a row and make enemy contact. Then we could go for a few weeks without any enemy contact. There was a lot of uncertainty. Every day was a new day, and we just didn't know what the results of it would be."

An example during Darryle's first tour perfectly illustrated this concept: "During that Tet Offensive, we were out in the field outside Hué, and we watched as the Vietnamese flag went down and the NVA flag went up."

That meant that the enemy had control of the city. The enemy had the strategic advantage. It was a low point in the war. But he hadn't lost his faith in the US military. And that feeling was justified. A short time later, American Marines went into Hué and retook the city.

For the Lord your God is He who goes with you, to fight for you

against your enemies, to save you.

—DEUTERONOMY 20:4

God's Voice in Battle

Shortly after witnessing that major victory, Darryle and his platoon again came under fire in an ambush. Soldiers were dying. Amid chaos and a fierce firefight, while running down a trail, Darryle felt God speak to him.

"We were taking fire, and I was on this hillside," Darryle recalled. "And I think that I either had a vision or I was knocked out. But I came to in this kind of visionary state. We were running down trails. I'd been up on top of the hill.

"God was talking to me, directing me which way to go. And I looked over this hill, and it had to be a dream or a vision: on the left side was hell. On the right side was heaven. I had to make a quick decision. *Which path to follow?* I went toward heaven, and I wasn't wounded. If I went the other way, maybe I would have been killed. I don't know that to be a fact—I just know that I had this warm feeling, and I was told to go to the right. And that's the way that I went—and I lived through that day.

"It was almost like I was reborn," Darryle said. "After that, I started praying again. I had been so bitter. And I think that happens to a lot of soldiers. You get bitter and want revenge. Losing friends is such a shock and you go into almost an animalistic mode; all you want to do is shoot, shoot, shoot. I think that everybody went through something like that in Vietnam at one time or another. I know I did."

That moment changed Darryle's life forever. Not only did it save his life, but it restored his relationship with his Heavenly Father. Amid the thick of the vicious firefight and the unknown of the jungle, he undeniably felt the presence of God and His direction showing him which way to go. Darryle's bitterness and anger melted. He took solace in the Lord's embrace.

God's Hand

God had spoken to Darryle and gotten him back on the right path back to prayer and away from desperate anger, but that didn't prevent more challenges. The vision he experienced on the hillside was part of a pattern that Darryle noticed in Vietnam. The men grew in their faith the longer they were at war.

"Not a lot of guys professed their faith or went to church or visited with the chaplain at first," Darryle said. "Whenever one came in, a few of us would gather informally on a hillside. Since we weren't at a big base, everything was very informal. We had no chapel. And what I noticed was that the longer into our deployment we were, the more ambushes and near misses and casualties we took, the more guys would show up for those sessions with the chaplains."

The firefights continued in ferocity and in the devastating casualty numbers. But Darryle could see God's hand at work in battle. He experienced it firsthand.

"When I went on my second deployment, I was certain the enemy was going to do everything they could to kill me. It felt like it was inevitable that I was going to get shot," Darryle began. "And that was one of those periods when, for seven days straight, we had somebody get shot and wounded. I couldn't help but think my number was up.

"After that terrible week, we were out on a patrol and I was the second guy in our line moving forward. A rocket-propelled grenade was shot at us and exploded into a tree, and shrapnel from it hurt several guys behind me. I was left with a few little burn marks. It was that close, but I was safe.

"Then we got in a firefight, and the guy in front of me, Dennis, turned to me and told me that he was hit. He fell to the ground. I knew that he was dead.

"The firefight kept going on. The enemy was up on a hill firing down at us. They were hitting rocks on the ground and kicking them up. I could feel them hitting my face, it was that close. A lot of soldiers have those kinds of close calls."

The Armor of God

The day of Darryle's close call was April 9, 1969. After learning of other events that occurred that day, it became clear that Darryle wasn't alone—he told me many soldiers had God's hand protecting them that day.

Darryle explained more fully what he meant: "You have to understand this part of the story. The day before, we'd gotten a directive from command that us recon guys had to wear our helmets. Normally, we just wore a cap. We were usually out at night, and we didn't engage in much direct-action fighting, unless we were ambushed like we were when we lost Dennis that day.

"After that firefight was over, we were back walking the trail. A couple of two-man teams were left to care for the bodies of our dead and injured. As we were walking, I spotted a guy with a bandage on his head. I recognized him as Keith Smith. He was new to the unit, a quiet guy. I asked him what had happened to him. He showed me his helmet. Turns out, an RPG was fired and hit him in the helmet. It penetrated that shell and his skin. He had survived, obviously, but was still dazed and in pain. I told him that it was a good thing we'd gotten that directive. He agreed."

On that very, very difficult day, three men in the platoon were killed and seven were wounded. Ten of the nineteen were casualties. The complexity of combat means many things can be true at once; disastrous missions and catastrophic losses can occur simultaneously with miraculous survivals and near misses. The existence of pain and violence does not exclude God's presence. Part of Darryle's extraordinary yet typical Vietnam War infantry experience is that he richly experienced all of it, those myriad realities, suffering unbearable losses alongside bearing witness

141

to God's grace. Filled with certainty and questions, mourning and faith. A child of God.

The Veteran Soldier

Sometimes Darryle's unit was forced to go out on patrols shorthanded. Eventually replacements came in. Darryle noticed how their presence served as a reminder of the effects their long deployments had on them. "War changes you in lots of ways. When you first get there, you worry about your hygiene. You brush your teeth. You shave. You make sure you keep your clothes clean. As time goes on, you're not as concerned about that," he explained. "You make sure your weapons are clean. You make sure you have your hand grenades properly placed.

"And when new people come in, you look at them and they've got fresh uniforms. They're shaved clean. They may even smell of aftershave. And that's when you notice your own state. It was kind of like that when the chaplains came in. There didn't seem to be any kind of regular schedule to it. They'd pop in and out, and it was seldom on a Sunday. But they'd be there and they would smile, and that was a nice break from the same routine.

"With the new guys and the chaplains, it was funny to see how they weren't all skinny and they weren't battle-hardened. That was a good reminder, but still it seemed kind of strange too. They were worried about when their next meal was coming, but I had different priorities."

After being in-country for many months, it wasn't until Darryle looked in his shaving mirror that he realized just how much his appearance had changed. Appearances can be deceiving, but a toll was being taken on all of them. The long, difficult grind of a year's deployment required a tenacity most can't understand. But Darryle and his squad were up to the demands being made on them. It also helped that those in charge understood that the soldiers in combat needed some relief.

Hope and Entertainment

There was little anyone could do to take Darryle's mind completely away from the realities of combat and the Vietnam War. He did appreciate the special meals the soldiers received at holidays like Easter, Thanksgiving, and Christmas. That was when they got "real" food—turkey, ham, mashed potatoes—each a nice treat and variation from their usual rations. Even more than the food, any variation from the day-to-day routine was welcome. But it would take something pretty special for him and his buddies to really take notice. So in December 1968, when they learned that the comedian and film star Bob Hope and his entourage of entertainers were coming to visit the troops, they eagerly looked forward to it. That was pretty special!

From 1964 to 1972, Bob Hope took nine trips to Vietnam. Darryle was there to see him and his fellow entertainers in 1967.

After the bombing of Pearl Harbor on December 7, 1941, Bob Hope wanted to host a show for service members and give back to the men and women serving in the US military. In 1942, while visiting servicemembers in Alaska, Hope told reporters: "Yes, Hollywood won't see so much of Hope from here on out. I've got other plans."

So began fifty-seven tours with the USO, from 1941 to 1991, where Hope entertained the troops in every major conflict from World War II through Operation Desert Storm.

According to the Vietnam Veterans Memorial Fund, one servicemember recalled: "Hope was funny, treating hordes of soldiers to roars of laughter. He was friendly—he ate with servicemen, drank with them, read their doggerel, listened to their songs. Hence boys whom Hope might entertain for an hour anticipated his arrival for weeks. And when he came, anonymous guys who had no other recognition felt personally remembered."

Hope's unwavering support for the troops earned him the unique privilege of being named an Honorary Veteran by the Secretary of Veterans Affairs in 1997, the only individual in history to have earned this honor.

"I was in Cu Chi at the time doing some training. We got a Christmas meal, but the big treat was the show. Not so much Bob Hope, but the pretty girls," said Darryle, laughing. "We talked about them for months after. Raquel Welch was with him. So was Barbara McNair, Miss World [Madeleine Hartog-Bel], and a few others, but it was those two beautiful women I mostly remember.

April 10th

Dear Mom & Dad,
    Well you'll never guess where I'm
writing this letter. At least I don't think
so. I'm at the 22nd Surg in Phu Bai. Simply
put I'm in the hospital. I don't know if they
write & tell you of these things or not. But
anyway about 12 o'clock on the 9th, we were
on a patrol in the A Shau Valley going up
this hill when we got hit. Me and the
guy right beside me we near the end &
we were running up to the front to help
out when all of sudden a big explosion
went off to our immediate side, About
1 foot from us. It was an RPG. An RPG
is an rocket like thing but is shot from the
shoulder. Something like an M72 LAW of the
Americans only better. Anyway we both got
hit by shrapmental. He got 6 real tiny
pieces - 2 in arm, 3 in leg, 1 in forehead.
I only got 1 piece but it was big, about
3/4 of an inch square. right in the back of
the head. It went right through my helmet.
Couldn't get Medivaced until this morning
because of the fog. So got here and they
operated, ha ha, that's what they called it too.
And I'm in the hospital. The doctor said that
with out my helmet I would have been killed
because the piece would have went into my
brain. So I'm just thanking the lord that it
wasn't to bad. So don't worry or anything
I'll be alright I guess. Right now I got

my head all bandage up and I'm going to get a little ghost time in. I'm suppose to go down south pretty soon. Don't know how far. At least to Da Nang maybe Chu Lai to the hospital the to recuperate & have it stitched up. Might miss R&R but doubt it. The Colonel was even here to see us this afternoon. But any way I showed today for the first time in 9 days and took a shower for the first time in over a month and am lying in a bed for the first time in over 4 months. I doing pretty good, got a head ache & a little dizzyness but feel real good. Doctor said it stopped just after it hit the bone & said most had been going thron got it so the Lord really was watching over me. I needed a rest any way ha ha. Haven't been getting any mail but 3 letters in the last 14 days & it was about that long ago since got mail and won't get now neither I suppose. But showed have a lot when I get out.

How is every thing back in Iowa? I hope fine. Well I'll try to write often & keep you posted. But I'm keeping the faith so keep praying and writing.

Love Keith

Beds sure are nice!!

Darryle's fortunate brother in arms, Keith Smith, writing home to his parents after surviving an RPG hit to his helmet.

"That show absolutely did boost our spirits and raised morale. But even at other times, if we were out in the field and not a big fire base, they tried to do something for us around the holidays. A hot meal was always a good thing. But out in the field, even on holidays we were busy and didn't think about what day it was much. We didn't think about what we were missing at home, or think that we wished we were home. We thought that every day.

"But, still, that USO Bob Hope show, that sure stayed with us," Darryle said, smiling.

The Service Continues

Darryle's service to this country has never stopped, continuing for decades after the last time he wore his combat fatigues in battle. He is an ambassador for the esteemed National Veterans Memorial and Museum in Columbus, Ohio. He is an active organizer for regular reunions with Vietnam veterans, and has worked tirelessly to ensure their contribution stays fresh in the nation's memory.

His daughter lives in Washington, DC, and Darryle visits there quite often. He makes sure to do one thing traditionally every time he's in town. "I go to the Vietnam Wall. I go first thing in the morning," Darryle said. "I get the largest cup of coffee that I can, and I sit on the knoll and drink it with all fifty-eight thousand of them. I do that because I remember what it was like when I was in Vietnam. We didn't have much water. Guys in my squad would take one canteen cap and fill it with water. We'd then all contribute coffee and creamer and put it in there. We'd then share it among us. Take a sip and pass it along. Then we'd go out on patrol—and maybe the next day, all of those same guys might not be there."

* * *

We are all there with him now—and with all Vietnam veterans. As Americans drink their morning cups of coffee throughout the country, I pray we all have them on our minds and in our hearts. Vietnam veterans like Darryle endured the unthinkable during one of the bloodiest conflicts in history, a war that threatened to tear apart our nation and left so many thousands of soldiers with lifelong trauma. Darryle embodies the bravery, dedication, and grace those young soldiers displayed during the long years of that fierce war. His compassion for his brothers in arms is outweighed only by the purity of his faith in Jesus Christ and his conviction that God never left his side.

We Americans are able to go about our day safe and secure, knowing that people like Darryle and the rest of Rubicon Platoon are still out there, the eyes and ears of our defense forces, the guardians of our freedom, protected by the Lord.

The Lord is my protector; he is my strong fortress.
My God is my protection, and with Him I am safe.

—PSALM 18:2

My great-grandfather, who served a remarkable career in
the US Army from 1912 to 1946. He saw action in Veracruz,
Mexico, was wounded in World War I, and continued
serving through World War II.

Then–Lieutenant Colonel Tim Karcher after a six-hour clearance operation with the Iraqi Army's 2nd Brigade, searching for insurgents and weapons caches in Baqubah, Iraq, December 2006.

(Courtesy of Tim Karcher)

The moment Tim reunited with his wife and daughters for the first time after an IED took his legs (and his life, before resuscitation), on board a medevac on a tarmac in Texas, August 2009.

(Courtesy of US Army)

Then-Sergeant Jeff Struecker reuniting with his wife, Dawn, upon his return to the US from Somalia, shortly after the Battle of Mogadishu, late October 1993.

(Courtesy of Jeff Struecker)

Sergeant First Class/18 Zulu Jeremiah Wilber while serving in 3rd Special Forces Group (Airborne) as an 18E at Fort Bragg (now Fort Liberty) in North Carolina, October 2014.

(Courtesy of Jeremiah Wilber)

Jeremiah's mother, Louise "Mountain Lamb" Wilber, posing for the famous Western artist Vel Miller, Montana, 1984.

(Courtesy of Jeremiah Wilber)

Jeremiah's father, Rick Wilber, bear hunting in Madison River Valley, Montana, Fall 1983.

(Courtesy of Jeremiah Wilber)

Lieutenant Colonel Anthony Randall (*top row, third from right*) and the ministry team of the Airborne and Ranger Training Brigade at Fort Benning (now Fort Moore) in Georgia, 2015. *(Courtesy of Anthony Randall)*

Anthony about to do one of the things he loves best besides ministering: jump out of an aircraft, Fort Liberty, North Carolina, 2012.

(Courtesy of Anthony Randall)

Lieutenant Commander Chris Baker (my second cousin) and his wife, Lieutenant Commander Angie Baker, in front of one of their birds, a P-3, Naval Air Station Whidbey Island, Washington, 2003.

(Courtesy of Chris and Angie Baker)

Angie and Chris as copilots for a P-3C Orion flight, despite being in different squadrons (all thanks to a "super-cool skipper"), 2003.

(Courtesy of Chris and Angie Baker)

Chris receiving the Lockheed Martin Wing Ten Aviator of the Year award with Angie next to him, Naval Air Station Whidbey Island, Washington, 2001.

(Courtesy of Chris and Angie Baker)

Sergeant First Class Jessica Harris at the Western Regional Counterdrug Training Center, Washington, 2011.

(Courtesy of Jessica Harris)

Jessica and teammates just before a convoy mission supporting Charlie Troop 1-303rd Cavalry Regiment, Iraq, 2008.

(Courtesy of Jessica Harris)

Jessica training with law enforcement as part of the National Guard Counterdrug Program, Washington, 2010.

(Courtesy of Jessica Harris)

Chaplain Doug Collins reuniting with his son Cameron after a deployment to Iraq, 2009.

(Courtesy of the Gainesville Times*)*

Chaplain Collins, prior to deploying to Balad, Iraq, speaking with Airman Christina Nissen in a C-17 Globemaster, December 2008.

(Courtesy of US Air Force)

Captain Charlie Plumb being welcomed home following his release after 2,103 days held in captivity by the North Vietnamese, February 18, 1973.

(Courtesy of TSGT Eddie P. Boaz / US Army)

A photo Darryle took of Second Squad, Recon Platoon, E Company 2/101st Airborne Division pausing in the Tam Dao mountain range north of Hanoi, February 1968.

(Courtesy of Darryle Endfinger)

Sergeant Major Darryle Endfinger and Platoon Sergeant First Class John David Henry of the Recon Platoon E Company 2/501st Airborne Division, shortly before the Tet Offensive, January 10, 1969.

(Courtesy of Darryle Endfinger)

Colonel Tom Moe (*third from right*) with fellow POWs, after he spent five years, one month, and twenty-two days in captivity, walking toward the aircraft that will fly them home, Gia Lam Airport, Vietnam, March 1973.

(Courtesy of Tom Moe)

Tom with his F-4 Phantom II; he flew eighty-four successful combat missions before an aircraft explosion led to his capture by the North Vietnamese, Da Nang Air Base, Vietnam, 1967.

(Courtesy of Tom Moe)

Tom reuniting with his wife, Chris, after five years as a POW as his daughter Connie looks on, Wright-Patterson Air Force Base, Ohio, March 18, 1973.

(Courtesy of Tom Moe)

Master Sergeant Robert Burr, at age twenty, posed for this photo while on R&R in Japan.

(Courtesy of Robert Burr)

Robert in his later years wearing his Military Order of the Purple Heart regalia.

(Courtesy of Ohio Department of Veterans Services)

Anton in a rare moment on land, after serving on a submarine, supply ship, hospital ship, and river gunboat, during Cooks and Bakers School, Class III, San Diego, California, 1939.

(Courtesy of Katherine Bertsch Compagno and Judy Baker)

Chief Commissary Steward Anton Lorenz (my great-cousin) with his wife, Gertrude, and their children, Geri and John, only months after the US Navy Yard at Pearl Harbor and Kaneohe Bay Naval Air Station were attacked while they were home on base at Kaneohe Bay, Oahu, Hawaii, 1942.

(Courtesy of Katherine Bertsch Compagno and Judy Baker)

Corporal Howard Spurlock (*far right*) posing with other members of the "Wolfhounds" near Pusan, 1951.

(*Courtesy of Howard Spurlock*)

Sergeant Andy Negra (*left*) with a fellow Super Sixth brother-in-arms during their long advance, which began on Utah Beach on July 18, 1944, carried through the Battle for Brest and the Battle of the Bulge, and ended in Germany after the liberation of the Buchenwald concentration camp, circa 1944.

(*Courtesy of Andy Negra*)

Members of the 128th Armored Field Artillery Battalion, 6th Armored Division during their advance in France or Germany, circa 1944–45.

(*Courtesy of Andy Negra*)

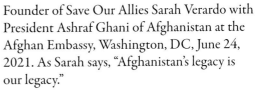

Founder of Save Our Allies Sarah Verardo with President Ashraf Ghani of Afghanistan at the Afghan Embassy, Washington, DC, June 24, 2021. As Sarah says, "Afghanistan's legacy is our legacy."

(Courtesy of Sarah Verardo)

Sarah with her husband, Sergeant Michael Verardo, at Walter Reed National Military Medical Center, where Mike has undergone over one hundred surgeries for his polytraumatic conditions resulting from his massive combat injuries, Washington, DC, 2019.

(Courtesy of Sarah Verardo)

Sarah, Mike, and their three daughters during Wounded Heroes Day ceremonies, Charlotte, North Carolina, April 24, 2024. On April 24, 2010, Mike barely survived his second of two IED explosions in two weeks in Afghanistan. Eleven years later, Wounded Heroes Day became an official state holiday in North Carolina, honoring Mike and his fellow wounded warfighters every year on that day.

(Courtesy of Sarah Verardo)

Sergeant Gabriel De Roo with his son, Gabriel Glen De Roo II, who was born during the six-month gap between his two deployments to Iraq, early 2006.

(Courtesy of Hannah Clark)

Gabriel made the Ultimate Sacrifice on August 20, 2006, killed by sniper fire in Mosul, Iraq. His funeral service was held at Temple Baptist Church in Tacoma, Washington, on August 30, 2006.

(Courtesy of Hannah Clark)

Command Sergeant Major Tom Satterly and his wife, Jen, cofounders and CEOs of the All Secure Foundation, which is dedicated to helping special operators and their families heal from the trauma of war in mind, body, and spirit, because true healing cannot exist without restoring the spirit.

(Courtesy of Tom and Jen Satterly)

Tom and Jen at a special operations fundraiser for suicide prevention in 2017.

(Courtesy of Tom and Jen Satterly)

Morgan (*center*) as an ensign during Naval Intelligence Officer Basic Course Phase I training, Virginia Beach, 2014.

(Courtesy of Morgan Ortagus)

Lieutenant Morgan Ortagus (*third from left*) eating dinner at the dining facility in the Green Zone after Friday evening Shabbat service, Baghdad, Iraq, 2007.

(Courtesy of Morgan Ortagus)

My great-great-aunt Lieutenant Luella Lorenz, US Army Nurse Corps, served with the 125th Evacuation Hospital as an anesthetist nurse, deploying to Europe for sixteen months beginning December 9, 1944.

(Courtesy of Katherine Bertsch Compagno)

Yours truly as a University of Washington US Air Force Reserve Officers' Training Corps (ROTC) cadet, 1998. I peaked at receiving the Cadet of the Quarter award.

(Courtesy of Katherine Bertsch Compagno)

Anton (Luella's cousin) on Yangtze River Patrol, in 1925. On March 31, 1946, after over twenty-two years of service, he retired with the rank of Chief Commissary Steward.

(Courtesy of Katherine Bertsch Compagno)

My father, Commander John Compagno, in 1975. He was a pathologist in the US Navy Medical Corps and served at the Armed Forces Institute of Pathology in Washington, DC, and the Oak Knoll Naval Hospital in Oakland, California (where I was born).

My mother and family historian, Katherine Bertsch Compagno, at the 42nd Rainbow Division Memorial at Croix Rouge Farm, France, in 2015, after visiting the grave of her great-uncle, Private First Class Joseph Lorenz, who died in WWI while fighting in the Rainbow Division and lays buried in Suresnes.

(Courtesy of Katherine Bertsch Compagno)

Me under the hood of a Black Hawk, Iraq, 2009. My signature joined that of many other celebrities and professional athletes who had visited our brave troops, representing the support of a nation for those so far from home.

"TEAM-C" NFL Raiderettes Tiphanie, Meena, Ashlee, Cole, and me (*left to right*), at a FOB with soldiers just returned from a foot patrol, Iraq, 2009.

My great-grandfather William Archibald Bertsch (*far left*) on Christmas Day in 1918. Born in 1895, he served in the US Army from 1912 to 1946 and saw action in Veracruz, Mexico, in World War I, and on through World War II, before finally retiring from the US Army Air Corps after a lifetime of service.

(Courtesy of Katherine Bertsch Compagno)

William (*center, back row*), with fellow members of the US Army 3rd Division, "Rock of the Marne," 4th Infantry. On July 24, 1918, a shell exploded underneath William while advancing in Jaulgonne, France. He lay in a coma for one month with serious injuries, during which the US Army could not identify him and sent his wife, Rosa (Joe and Lou's sister), a telegram that he was presumed dead! A corrected telegram arrived weeks later. William's Purple Heart medal hangs proudly in our family home.

(Courtesy of Katherine Bertsch Compagno)

Luella, or Aunt Lou, at one of the field hospitals; her first surgical assignment was a leg amputation. She said her motto was "I walk in my own shoes and at my own pace."

(Courtesy of Katherine Bertsch Compagno)

Aunt Lou in Aachen, Germany, 1945. One letter home reassured her family: "Don't worry. As I sit here, the walls are the same, the boys speak my language, the sky is the same blue, the rain is just as wet and the snow just as white."

(Courtesy of Katherine Bertsch Compagno)

Despite my great-grandfather's impressive military decorations,
we are especially proud of his Commendation Medal, awarded
after he saved a drowning woman in the Mad River in Dayton,
Ohio. Both his WWI Purple Heart and the Commendation Medal
hang reverently on our walls.

Colonel Tom Moe about to board his F-4 fighter
jet in Danang, Vietnam, circa 1968.

10

The Strength to Endure

Colonel Tom Moe,
US Air Force (Retired),
Five-Year Prisoner of War

On January 16, 1968, Colonel Tom Moe was at the controls of his F-4 Phantom II, flying his eighty-fifth combat mission in the Vietnam War. An overwhelming thirteen F-4 pilots had lost their lives in just one week. Not from enemy fire. They had all been flying the same missions with the same ordnance on board—and it was their own munitions that had exploded prematurely. All Phantoms were grounded temporarily while the US Air Force attempted to identify the fuse issue.

Colonel Moe's flight was the first combat mission since. The pilots had been assured the frightening, fatal issue had been resolved. Suddenly, an explosion ripped through the air. The fuse on the ordnance of his wingman had sparked, engulfing both jets in flames. Colonel Moe had to eject over North Vietnam. He exchanged gunfire with the enemy while parachuting down. Surviving the firefight, he landed safely in the jungle and, for two full days, evaded detection by the Viet Kong.

Colonel Moe was then captured. He spent the next five years, one month, and twenty-two days as a prisoner of war. This is his story of unwavering strength.

The Right Stuff

Before entering the military, Colonel Tom Moe planned on entering seminary to become a Lutheran pastor. Instead, he heeded another calling: to follow in his family's footsteps and enlist. His father had seen combat in World War II in Okinawa, Japan. A cousin had been murdered by the North Koreans during that war. He wanted to honor his family's legacy going all the way back to the Revolutionary War: to serve and defend this great country.

After three years as a member of the United States Naval Construction Battalions (the Seabees), he had a choice: do what he had set his heart on—become an aviator—or listen to what another major chamber of his heart told him to do. His then-girlfriend (spoiler alert: now his wife of fifty-nine years) knew that the attrition rate among Navy pilots was high.

Tom got the girl and the gig. He enlisted in the US Air Force Reserve in 1964 and received his commission through the Air Force ROTC program in 1965. "The war was on. The assignment I had was known as a 'pipeline assignment,'" Tom told me. "You get your wings and you're off to war, boom, just like that—at twenty-three years old."

That was his entrée into the Vietnam War. His squadron's mission was air-to-ground, dropping bombs on the Ho Chi Minh Trail. This was the name American military personnel gave to the vital supply route of roads and trails through which troops and matériel traveled.

It was a high-risk mission, but surprisingly, the gravest danger came from within. The modified bombs they dropped were designed to lie on the ground and have their vibration-sensitive fuses be set off by passing trucks. Unfortunately, they were malfunctioning and going off while still attached to the aircraft in flight.

"Prior to November of '67, I'd carried hundreds of bombs with those fuses without incident," Tom said. "We knew that it was a matter of time. So, that January day, we took off thinking that we weren't going to get through it, or the pilots and aircraft behind us weren't going to. Sure enough, one of those fuses went off on my wingman's airplane. The force of the explosion took both of us out of the air. I was immediately angry. Here we were going against an enemy that was shooting at us, and our own ordnance knocked us out of the air. Miraculously, all four of us aboard the two aircraft survived."

Tom ejected from the aircraft. To hear him tell this riveting story is an experience in and of itself. Even after all these years, he still has the cool and calm of a fighter pilot.

His remarkable composure is just as inspiring as his resolve and bravery. Throughout his story, he maintained that unflappable demeanor that reinforces why, indeed, fighter pilots like Tom have all the right stuff.

Cool, Calm, Captured

There is another aspect to the miracle of his survival. His explosion—or more specifically, his quick thinking afterward—saved the other pilots' lives. "I'm coming down on my parachute from twenty-five thousand feet. I got on my survival radio and got a hold of another flight and said, 'Look, I don't know if I'm going to get out of here. So you need to pass the word down the line that those bomb fuses are bad.' I learned, six years later, they immediately turned around those other flights which had those bombs aboard. The four of us were the first to survive one of those incidents. Eventually, the Air Force figured out what the problem was with those fuses. Us having that malfunction ultimately saved a few lives."

Although his life hung in the balance while dangling from the parachute, Tom's commitment to warning the others reveals both his impeccable quick thinking and his selfless servant's heart, two qualities he maintained throughout captivity.

Indestructible Faith

Tom was held in solitary confinement. While he briefly felt sorry for himself in the early days, those feelings didn't last long. Tom credited this shift—and his ability to endure overwhelming pain and fear—to his faith. "Faith is powerful. And by faith, I don't mean the kind where you're ready for the golden light to come down from heaven. For me, faith meant having the strength to face whatever. I know in my heart that there are objective truths. I try to live by those truths. Faith gives us the strength to live by those truths—to know right from wrong."

Tom described captivity as a roller-coaster ride. "I don't mean just the feeling sorry for myself part—that was a brief phase. Anger was a part of it as well. I was very angry at the people holding us. What those captors did to us, murdering prisoners, beating them to death. They almost beat me to death. What I found through those experiences was the peace I got from my faith in God."

Tom prayed for strength. "Sure, I also prayed for the door to be opened so that I could go home. I wanted to see my wife and my little girl, my parents. Mostly, though, I prayed for strength." He needed faith to endure, especially during nightmarish torture sessions. Like when he was "tied up like a pretzel," handcuffed with a pole behind his elbows and a gag in his mouth. With his legs held in irons and his neck tied to those metal restraints, he was brutally kicked by a guard wearing heavy boots until he passed out from the pain.

Tom developed a coping mechanism for the beatings that scared him a little too. He could elevate from his body, looking down at what was happening to him. Going there enabled him to deal with the pain, but he feared he might not return. He also based his mental fantasy not on retreating from the pain, but on real things. He designed and built homes, about ten of them, some of them dream houses, some more practical. Laying the cement, putting up the two-by-fours, driving each nail, sawing each board—no minute detail escaped Tom's mind, as he escaped the horrific pain. And with that mental exercise came resolve. This would *not* be where he cashed it in, he vowed.

One of the many drawings Mike McGrath created
depicting the life of American POWs in Vietnam.

Tom also knew he wasn't alone, many POWs were unimaginably worse off than he was. One friend, Captain Mike McGrath, had a horrible open fracture that went untreated. Mike used ripped pajamas tied to the leg of his wooden bed, leaning back to get the bone back inside his flesh, passing out over and over in agony until he succeeded. There is seemingly no end to the horrors these men endured at the hands of the torturous guards.

Tom and Mike have remained close friends since their captivity. Mike is renowned for the pen-and-ink drawings he produced after he was released. Some are graphic depictions of the horrible conditions and treatment. He has been the subject of numerous television interviews, including an episode of the PBS series *American Experience*.

Tom and his fellow POWs all remain big parts of one anothers' lives. "Our fraternity is as solid as you can ever imagine. We love each other," Tom said. "When we're together, we just sit around and tell stories. And when my family has joined us, they comment, 'All you guys do is laugh!' They wonder how we can have anything funny from those days to say."

While their bodies were breakable, their faith was indestructible. No torture, no pain, could dampen their faith that carried them through. Not only in God, but in more: "The spirit we developed came from our faith individually, and also our faith in each other. Faith in our families. We had faith that our government would, eventually, make things happen in a good way. And even if we don't survive in the sense of living through it, we can survive by never losing our faith."

Saving Each Other

Tom never lost faith, but he nearly lost his life. After one of the worst periods of torture had ended, Tom was tended to by his cellmate. Lieutenant Colonel Myron Donald's own body was so ravaged by dysentery, "If the guy turned sideways, he wouldn't cast a shadow." Tom's face was so disfigured from the beatings that Myron didn't recognize him when the guards brought him back into the cell. His broken ribs needed to be set back in place and bound. His kidneys needed time to heal. Weak, exhausted, and starving, Tom was on the knife edge between surviving and dying.

Myron knew that as weak as he was, Tom was worse. While their rations were meager—a bowl of weak soup and a small crust of hard bread, barely enough to sustain a healthy person—Myron began giving his share of food to Tom.

Tom credits Myron's sacrifice with saving his life. Myron, Tom says, would disagree, arguing that it was Tom who saved his. Likely both are right, and both are true. Tom's former cellmate Captain Dennis Chambers had horrible asthma and would lie on the floor gasping for breath. Tom would describe palm trees swaying in the breeze, the

Former American POWs
celebrating their freedom
aboard the aircraft
bringing them home.

ocean lapping on the beach, telling him stories to keep him distracted. And alive. "How he didn't suffocate from asthma in that dense jungle humidity, I'll never know. But he didn't." They still talk every day.

How the American POWs supported and saved one another through their years of suffering is one of most inspiring stories in modern warfare. These men were brothers through and through.

Standing Tall

The Americans were committed to defying their captors, employing hunger strikes and using other tools of resistance. Tom paid a heavy price for refusing to participate in the enemy's propaganda. He was forced to stand immobile or kneel in excruciating pain for hours around the clock, and was beaten "to a pulp" by twenty guards in turn. He was waterboarded. Tom felt himself drowning. As he passed out, thinking he was dying, his last thought was *Thank God we are making a stand against this kind of society.*

In the midst of this inhumanity there was some mercy. Once, when placed in the pretzel position overnight, Tom heard the dreaded sounds of footsteps and the jangling of keys. He steeled himself. "One of the less hostile guards sneaked in and loosened the ropes a little. If he hadn't, I'm sure I would have lost both arms. In that case I would have vanished with the other badly injured POWs who were never repatriated."

The respite was brief. Other guards returned and began slamming Tom's head into the concrete floor, telling Tom, It's easy to die but hard to live. *We'll show you how hard!*

"My prayers became desperate gasps," Tom said. "The only solution was to stop living, but what can you do when you're tied up? You can't will your heart to stop beating." Tom didn't stop resisting their demands for a "confession." The enemy didn't stop their ferocious beatings.

Then, suddenly, the torture stopped. Tom knows the Viet Cong weren't being humanitarian; they were being strategic. Their odds of winning the war were low and they wanted support from the rest of the world. Killing and torturing POWs needed to end. Tom survived but had nearly joined the distressing ranks of those who died in captivity.

An Unexpected Gift

As much as their bodies needed nourishment, so did their souls. Improbably, there was one extraordinary day where their souls were fed. Until that point they were ridiculed for their faith, regardless of denomination. The men were mocked during torture

Colonel Tom Moe's wife, Chris, appearing with Bob Hope
on the *Phil Donahue Show.* They were seeking support for American
personnel who were MIA and POWs.

sessions: *God's not going to come take you out of this prison!* "Religions didn't divide us," Tom said. "We were united."

"The greatest moment—the most emotional moment—came one Christmas Eve. The door opened on all these big cells. In came the guard with a Bible, a chunk of bread, and a bottle of wine. *Here you are.*"

He was offering them the opportunity for Communion. "Communion is a very special thing that's conducted by ordained priests and ministers. And we had Jews in the room. We had at least one atheist. *What do we do and how do we do this?* We didn't have anyone to proclaim forgiveness. No one to consecrate the bread and the wine since we had no ordained people. So, we voted. And to the man, we agreed to hold a Communion service," Tom said. "Why? Because Communion is an act of forgiveness. And if we were screwing this up, God would forgive us."

They decided they needed to decorate the white walls of their cells: "Somebody had a red blanket, somebody had a blue blanket. We hung those in the back. So we had red, white, and blue." Then they began this special ceremony.

One by one, every man stood up and recited something from their church services. "Because I originally went to seminary, I had some memories from the liturgy of the Lutheran Church and a few chants: the Gloria Patri [Glory Be to the Father] and some others. I sang them; I used to have a voice," Tom shared. "One of our Jewish brothers got up and chanted some pieces from his service. And every one of us participated in the bread and wine." It was a special spark in the long years of darkness.

Christianity is simple. It is about love. It is about fellowship. It is about brothers in a room who seemingly have nothing—but have faith. At the time of year when we celebrate the birth of our Savior and God's unending love for us, the root of our eternal salvation, those imprisoned men had one profound moment of spiritual freedom. Against all odds, that special Christmas Eve, a group of blessed men who were being persecuted received Communion.

In Some Minutes

On March 14, 1973, as part of Operation Homecoming after the Paris Peace Accords of 1973 had been signed, Tom and a large group of prisoners were part of a negotiated release. Over the preceding year, Tom had been especially anxious. The approximately six hundred prisoners held in the so-called Hanoi Hilton had been dispersed to smaller camps. Tom was relocated near the Chinese border and that was especially nerve-racking. "If things went sour, we were right on the border, and it would take nothing to get us moved across it into China," he explained.

One day, the men were loaded into flatbed trucks and taken back to Hanoi. For years the men had discussed this: When it came time to be released, they wanted the first shot down and captured to be the first released. First in, first out. They swore to themselves they would adhere to that order.

In the later winter of 1973, it seemed as if they were going to get their wish to go home. But the order was To Be Determined. The men were placed in smaller camps, and among Tom's group, they had all been shot down within months of one another. Their pact was assured. Just as their captivity was a roller coaster, so, too was their wait to be released. Their guards had become more lenient. Rations increased. They were allowed to spend time out in the sun. One day, in mid-February, an American C-141 transport plane was even spotted in the sky.

Still, the wait dragged on, made all the more frustrating with incessant propaganda being played over the camp radio, reminding them that they were war criminals and would actually never be set free.

One of the running jokes among the prisoners was that no matter what they asked their guards for, they would be told—whether their request was granted or not—that it would be there "in some minutes." For a group of prisoners, some of whom had been held as long as nine years, that was a lot of minutes to wait for what they all hoped for: to be set free. And in a small but mighty moment of triumph, the men turned that phrase into a symbol of their unwavering strength.

Winning

On March 13, 1973, all of the men were gathered together. The prison camp's commander came forward. "He didn't speak English, so we had a translator. He read the release document that was negotiated in Paris. And we're told we're going to go home the next day. And then the camp planner—of course he's got on his big smiley face—said, 'Now go back to your rooms and take some buckets of water and clean out the rooms.'"

Tom, laughing, told me, "There was a movie camera up in this second story of a building, so we're all doing obscene gestures. And then one of the prisoners, Brigadier General Bud Day—what a hero he was—walked up to the camp commander and looked him up and down. And he said about the cleanup order: '*In some minutes!*'

"Then we all walked back to our cells, and we didn't clean up anything. Little moments of triumph." Triumph indeed.

The next morning, they were escorted into a large room where they could pick out clean civilian clothes. They defied orders regarding what and how much they could take back with them. They also refused to give in to other aspects of the suddenly amiable Viet Cong captors. They were loaded on the bus to take them to the airport, from where they would eventually fly home. The bus made a brief stop where their smiling enemies offered them beer and bananas. None of the soon-to-be former POWs took them. Later, the men saw their chief torturer sitting at a table along with other Western and Asian delegates.

They repeated what they'd said to that vile person many times during his torture sessions: "*We're going home some day, but you have to stay here.*" Sweet freedom was here at last.

At the airport, Tom and the rest of the men conducted themselves with honor and dignity. Tom was most impressed by how well trained they all were, how disciplined. Many of these men had endured much longer stretches of being held in isolation—some for as long as two, three, and four years. But they all behaved the same. They were lined up four abreast, and they no longer displayed obscene gestures or any other signs of ill discipline, collectively refusing to do anything to dishonor themselves or their country. Tom recalls them all being called by name by a one-star general before boarding the C-141 transport.

Free

And then the plane lifted off. The Americans were headed home. After a few moments, the pilot announced they were "feet wet"—they were over the ocean. The men erupted into shouts of joy, rejoicing, a collective celebration. "I experienced this unreal oneness," Tom shared.

They were free.

*   *   *

In total, North Vietnam returned 591 POWs: 325 Air Force personnel, 77 Army, 138 Navy, 26 Marines, and 25 civilians. A total of 660 American military POWs survived the war.

Tom and his fellow POWs displayed extraordinary strength and perseverance in the face of prolonged untenable pain and suffering. These exceptional men resisted the enemy's efforts to degrade them, dehumanize them, and strip them of their faith in God. Their capacity to endure, like God's love for us, knew no bounds. Tom would never accept acknowledgment above or beyond any other American there; each man represented an individual tenacity and bravery in the face of torture, resolve in the face of impending death, and a commitment to each other as brothers that exceeded their own self-care. Even before capture, with the enemy closing in, Tom destroyed his radio—and thus all hopes for rescue—to ensure it wouldn't fall into enemy hands.

"You know, we always pray for a nice day if we're going to have a picnic. I don't think that's a serious prayer. . . . We hope. Maybe that's a better word. We hope for the best and we pray when we're faced with the worst. We pray for the strength to endure."

Tom indeed was faced with the worst. And he endured the worst through and by his faith. God answered Tom's prayer for the strength to endure.

Upon arriving home, Tom was awarded two Silver Stars.

Colonel Tom Moe's Silver Star Citation

First Lieutenant Thomas N. Moe distinguished himself by gallantry in connection with military operations against an opposing armed force as an F-4C pilot in Southeast Asia on January 16, 1968. On that date, Lieutenant Moe had to eject from his F-4C in North Vietnam over one hundred miles from friendly territory. He evaded capture for almost forty-eight hours, vectored search aircraft into his area, and called for air suppression against hostile forces at times within one hundred meters of his own position. When his capture seemed unavoidable, he destroyed his radio, isolating himself from rescue, rather than risk its capture and use to jeopardize the rescue of his fellow crew member. By his gallantry and devotion to duty, Lieutenant Moe has reflected great credit upon himself and the United States Air Force.

Therefore we do not lose heart. Though outwardly
we are wasting away, yet inwardly we are being renewed day by day.
For our light and momentary troubles are achieving for us an eternal
glory that far outweighs them all. So we fix our eyes not on what is seen,
but on what is unseen, since what is seen is temporary,
but what is unseen is eternal.

—2 CORINTHIANS 4:16–18

President Ronald Regan with US troops at Camp Liberty Bell in the demilitarized zone of South Korea in November 1983.

US Marines attending services to honor the fallen at the Masan Military cemetery in Korea on September 29, 1950.

Sergeant Robert
Burr, age twenty,
while on R&R in
Japan.

Corporal Howard Spurlock
credits God for having
guarded him through one
of the fiercest battles
in the Korean War.

11

All the Days Ordained for Me

Corporal Howard Spurlock, US Army (Retired)

Master Sergeant Robert Burr, US Army (Retired)

The tenor of the Korean War harkened back to World War I, with insidious trench warfare and hillside battles, unbearable weather conditions, scant communication with loved ones back home, and a global government engagement that felt far away from those brave boots on the ground. Ferocious battles lasting weeks took place in the frigid cold throughout the war.

From 1950 through 1953, sixteen United Nations member countries fought against North Korea, the People's Republic of China, and the Soviet Union to prevent the spread of communism. By July 1950, US troops were in combat against North Korea. Many US regiments saw repeated intense action, minor injuries subsumed within resolve as the forces continued their dogged fight that comprised the third largest world war.

Among these notorious battles were the Battle of Bloody Ridge, which lasted over three weeks with 2,700 casualties; the Battle of Heartbreak Ridge, lasting seventeen days with 3,700 American and French lives lost; and the Battle of Chosin Reservoir (also known as the Battle of Lake Changjin or the Chosin Reservoir Campaign), which lasted one month and saw a devastating 18,000 US casualties including 2,500 killed in action, 5,000 wounded, and almost 8,000 who suffered from frostbite.

Corporal Howard Spurlock was part of the US Army's 27th Infantry Regiment, 25th Infantry Division, known as the Wolfhounds. The Wolfhounds were an integral part of the success of the American forces alongside the South Koreans and NATO, fighting in several violent battles. Corporal Spurlock survived the Battle of Chosin Reservoir, against those disastrous odds, and was subsequently awarded the Silver Star, the United States' third-highest military decoration for valor in combat, for his "conspicuous gallantry and intrepidity" during the fiercest of the fights. He sustained permanent wounds and was also awarded the Purple Heart.

Master Sergeant Robert Burr, 2d Infantry Division, 38th Regiment, Company F, US Army, fought in both the Battle of Bloody Ridge—becoming squad leader after his was killed—and the brutal Battle of Heartbreak Ridge, just mere days apart. Master Sergeant Burr was wounded in Heartbreak Ridge, leaving part of himself there on the cold ground, subsequently receiving the Purple Heart.

These are their stories.

War Begins Again

Among those who fought in Korea, Howard Spurlock's path to the military is a familiar one. Born in May 1929 in Big Creek, Kentucky, the seventh of ten children raised during the Great Depression, Howard recalled that they were forced to eat nearly everything they raised on the farm. Just before Pearl Harbor, two of Howard's brothers were drafted and his father left to find work at a defense industry plant in Cincinnati. World War II was over, but the economic conditions and employment opportunities in rural Kentucky were not great. In 1948, Howard enlisted in the Army.

God Knows Us

In looking back on his time in Korea, Howard told me, "In those years, I wasn't walking in the way of Christ. But later, I could see that He knew me. He was guarding me. He knew where He was going to call me to. He kept me safe. He got me home. I did have to spend eighteen months in an Army hospital getting my hand rebuilt, but I survived the war."

Not only did Howard survive the war, but he survived one of its most memorable and terrible battles. Assigned to an artillery division, he was there to defend the 105 mighty Howitzers. Before leaving Fort Knox for Korea, Howard and the rest of those being deployed were told that the American troops had been advancing rapidly. They had left behind a few small pockets of resistance that they would have to address, but the war would soon be over. That was true until December 1950, when the Chinese entered the war.

"The first time we were shelled, I heard that screaming sound they make. We'd been told about it, but this [was] real," Howard said. "We were digging our fox holes when it came in. Instinct took over and I dropped to the ground and hugged Mother Earth. Some of our unit took a direct hit and they didn't stand a chance."

With the Chinese joining the fight, the Americans were in greater jeopardy than ever before: they were essentially cut off. Military command called in ships from the Navy's Seventh Fleet. Howard and other members of the brave Wolfhounds made it to a port city where "The Big Mo" waited: the mighty USS *Missouri*, which represented the greatest firepower the US had. "They turned loose everything they had," Howard said, "and they shelled the beach because the Chinese and the Koreans were right on our heels. We were taken south to Pusan, and then started our drive back North from there. Most of the activity was north of the 38th parallel at that time."

While on the move one night in February 1951, intelligence reports came in indicating they were going to be attacked that night. The company commander ordered Howard and others to move the warning flares that were a part of their perimeter defense farther away. While moving one, the flare exploded. The concussive effects knocked Howard to the ground, and as he put it, "things went a little fuzzy." He has vague recollections of being taken to a field surgical hospital and then to a hospital in Japan. He lost a thumb and forefinger and had other injuries to the bones in his hand, requiring multiple surgeries through the years.

Caring for Others

Upon returning home, Howard became a strong Christian, active in church and in his community. On the day I spoke with him, seven decades later, Howard glowed with faith. At a young ninety-five years old, Howard's citing of chapter and verse was as impressive as his spurt of energy.

Howard had recently been reading the Psalms, and he quoted these words from Psalm 139:61, inspired by the Holy Spirit: *"Your eyes saw my unformed body; all the days ordained for me were written in Your book before one of them came to me."*

The Armor of God is important to Howard. "I have seven different plastic cards, each one representing one piece of armor and I keep that in my Bible," he told me. "The main things, though, are simple: When Jesus was asked about the most important Commandments, He said, *Love the Lord your God with all your heart, soul, mind, and strength.* And the other one is to *love your neighbor as yourself.* The way I look at it, if we can meet that second one, we're going to fulfill all of the Commandments. And that's one way we can arm ourselves. If we see Satan trying to creep in and bring something to cause us to do less than love one another, then we should be on guard right away."

There is no better advice from this lighthouse of a man, this hero who fought so gallantly for democracy all those years ago.

A Bible in My Pocket

Master Sergeant Robert "Bob" Burr, US Army, wasn't particularly religious as a child. But in reflecting on his time fighting in Korea, it was clear God was with him, even if he wasn't yet with God.

"I had some pretty close experiences in Korea. One was early on. A small detachment of us were at this outpost miles from the line. We saw enemy troops on the road ahead of us. My squad leader tapped me on the helmet. He indicated that he was going to hide behind a wall. I fired at the enemy, and no sooner than I did, a machine gun opened up on us. My squad leader got hit. I didn't. That made no sense. I was standing there in the open with the skyline behind me. I was a beautiful target. He was behind a wall. But he gets hit. So, I became squad leader that day."

For many young men in the thick of war and battle, prayer at those times came from loved ones at home. "I carried a Bible in my pocket all the time," Bob continued. "I'm sure my grandmother's prayers had been answered that day."

The familiarity, the comfort, the connection of the Bible itself had an important impact on Bob. In retrospect, he felt that he should have attended the chaplain's services, but Bob benefited from having the Bible with him. "It felt so good to be able to relate to people back home. They were reading it and had in their hands the same thing I had in Korea."

And fundamentally, Bob knew Whose hands he was in. "I know that if it weren't for God, I wouldn't be here. He had it all planned out. I was where I was supposed to be. I did what I was supposed to do. God guided me through all of it."

Brotherhood

Bob fought in the notorious and fierce battle of Heartbreak Ridge. During the fight, an enemy shell exploded just behind him. He survived the blast, but the vicious effects on his body required immediate medical evacuation. "Immediate" in that war had a different practical application, however.

Bob told me he had fond memories of the evacuation, and after he explained why it makes perfect sense. After the difficult ambulance journey over rocky, mountainous terrain, he was loaded onto a train. And for someone who hadn't slept in a bed or showered for weeks and weeks, being able to lie down in clean white sheets was wonderful. So was being served hot food. "Seeing the pretty nurses didn't hurt either!" Bob playfully added.

What did hurt him was that the brotherhood he shared with other soldiers was frequently too brief. With replacements coming in and other men rotating out, he often found himself not recognizing those he fought alongside. Even worse, for Bob, was coming home and learning how many friends had been killed in action.

"I tried so hard to connect with one guy. I had joined the Veterans of Foreign Wars, and through connections got an address for him. I showed up at the door, only to be told by his mother that he had died in Korea. I hated that."

Bob "absolutely recommends" every soldier, present and future, carry a Bible with them. "The more help you can get the better," he told me. "It's like having a parachute. You don't have to have one, but if the plane goes down, you'll be glad you have it."

The wisest advice, from a blessed and brave hero, who fought with such valor and sacrificed so much for our freedom.

* * *

As of this writing, there are approximately 776,000 Korean War veterans still living, making up 4 percent of the total veterans' population. As this number inevitably decreases, so too do the opportunities to hear their stories firsthand, to serve as direct witnesses to their testimonies.

Our Korean War veterans saw ferocious trench and hillside combat while sustaining weeks without hearing from loved ones, all for a stated greater good that at times seemed illusive, and under the heavy cloud of prolonged armistice negotiations that enhanced politicization and threatened morale. And notably, the home front progressed with relatively minimal disruption. Unlike the terminations of the prior world wars, the Korean War veterans returned home to minimal celebration, minimal fanfare, and a federal government that had slashed the Veterans Affairs and GI Bill's budgets.

Many Korean War veterans thus encountered a woeful lack of resources and an isolation; while the government attempted to rectify that decades later, it did not assuage the pain the veterans endured at the time. Part of the miracle of God's enduring love for us is knowing when He is filling the gaps, knowing His living water sustains us outside of—or despite—insufficient earthly sustenance.

I pray these brave veterans like Howard and Bob feel the gratitude and love from their fellow Americans; that their stories are heard, validated, and celebrated as an irreplaceable part of our country's fabric; that their brotherhood endures far beyond their fleeting earthly chapters; and that their souls are lifted in the knowledge their earthly service and sacrifices were not in vain, and will never be forgotten.

I will be with you until the end of all days,
I will be with you until the end of all ages.

—MATTHEW 28:20

The SS *Leviathan* returns to Hoboken, New Jersey, with soldiers after World War I in 1918.

Easter morning services on the
Italian front, April 1944.

My great cousin Anton Lorenz,
US Navy Chief Commissary Steward.

Lieutenant Luella Lorenz, US Army Nurse,
125th Evacuation Hospital. She served in
England, France, and Germany, and was in
Germany when General Eisenhower declared
full victory attained in Europe.

Sergeant Andy Negra in France,
circa 1944.

12

The Greatest Generation

Sergeant Andrew Negra,
US Army (Retired)

Chief Commissary
Steward Anton Lorenz,
US Navy (Retired)

Lieutenant Luella
Lorenz Cochran,
US Army Nurse Corps
(Retired)

The generation that came of age in the 1940s came to be known as the "Greatest Generation," hallmarked by resilience, patriotism, and strength throughout World War II. Via selfless service and commitment to country, members of this generation fought and served abroad and participated in the war effort on the home front with clear-eyed dedication and unity for good. The success of America and the Allied Forces, against all odds, is attributed to these outstanding men and women. The following three very special individuals are no exception.

US Army Sergeant Andrew "Andy" Negra's service history reads as a remarkable lesson in American impact in World War II: beginning with landing on Utah Beach, Normandy, July 18, 1944, six weeks after D-Day, his "Super Sixth" Armored Division fought in the Battle of the Bulge; then the siege of Bastogne, Belgium; and helped liberate the Buchenwald concentration camp in April 1945. From growing up in small-town Pennsylvania coal country, attending Russian Orthodox church services, to being drafted and fighting for 233 straight days in brutal weather, his experiences cover the breadth of the war effort and show how ordinary Americans made extraordinary impact. His storytelling shines bright with his memories.

A Call to Action

On what started out to be just another December Sunday in 1941, after attending services at St. Ellien of Homs Orthodox Church, sixteen-year-old Andy Negra made his way to the only theater in Brownsville, Pennsylvania. It being winter, Andy decided against keeping to his usual routine—taking the dime his father had given him for the church offering, pocketing it, and spending a nickel on an ice cream cone and keeping the change. He did this while the sermon was being delivered and the Orthodox mass droned on in Russian. Andy, who is hale and hearty now at one hundred years old, smiled and winked as he shared that less-than-holy recollection.

Andy continued the story, the twinkle in his eye becoming a somber ember at the memory. "I don't recall the movie. I was up in the balcony. All of a sudden the movie stopped and the screen dimmed. This guy walked out in front, I think he must have been the manager, and said, 'The United States is at war with Japan. Japan has bombed Pearl Harbor, and we are at war with them. Everybody hear that?'

"Well, I know I did. I got up and ran home. It was scary. Then things settled down a bit and along came rationing and people were told to conserve and grow their Victory garden. It was just me and my dad at home. He was a pretty tough guy, abusive, didn't speak much English. My mom left him, and I loved him even though he treated me rough. And he had a rough life. Worked in the coal mine, got his pay on a Friday and went to the beer joint and took out his anger on whoever was home."

Despite the relative poverty in which the family lived and his parents' lack of education, Andy was determined to graduate from high school, and he did just that before being drafted into the Army in 1943. Following basic training he joined the 128th Armored Field Artillery Battalion, 6th Armored Division, known as the Super Sixth. His unit landed on Utah Beach in Normandy on July 18, 1944. They arrived six weeks after D-Day, the Allied invasion also known as Operation Overlord. That invasion contributed to the Allies' turning the tide of war against Nazi Germany and the Axis powers.

Andy recalled a chance meeting. "When we left England, we crossed the channel. As we landed, I heard somebody calling my name. I looked down and there was George Frank, a guy from my hometown. He was part of the crew that helped our boats get ashore there at Utah Beach. Those guys helped us get our tanks onto the beach. And off we went."

And off Andy and the rest of the Super Sixth went, half-track troop carriers and tanks, on a trek that would eventually lead them to Bastogne. First, they would have to cover 240 miles, and along the way they saw what the armored division had done in the weeks since D-Day.

"Once we landed, we went to a town call Sainte-Mère-Église. All our units formed up there, and our orders were to take Brest. That town was of real strategic importance."

A historically significant port in Brittany, France, Brest would prove crucial to establishing supply lines. All Andy knew was what his orders were.

The Unexpected

"The first thing you have to understand is that we were nineteen years old," Andy said. "We're still young, we were free and easy. We did things the way we wanted to. I wasn't scared because I didn't know what we're getting into. We moved along pretty okay, until we reached Avranches, another port city. I was riding along, and we heard the sound of aircraft, German Messerschmitt fighter planes. Our column stopped beneath a row of trees. I jumped out of the half-track and ran to an open field and hid behind a well. Those planes were firing their machine guns, strafing us. I'll never be able to figure out why, but instead of going after that entire column, they focused their fire on me. Fortunately, I was on the far side of the well, and the well got pretty shot up, but I was fine."

That was a close call, but they enjoyed another success—capturing a German general, Hans Speth. Andy and his troops were on their way to Brest to join the rumored number of between forty and sixty thousand soldiers. Fortunately, the armored division did its job. The men divided the enemy. However, circumstances foiled the Super Sixth's plan to take Brest. They were greatly outnumbered and were then directed to another target. It would take a month before US troops took Brest. Andy was assigned to work as a member of the survey team. From inside the tank, he consulted maps and helped plot the positions of German forces.

Andy and the Sixth spent 233 straight days fighting. After a brief break, word came down that they were going to face off against the Germans in what became known as the Battle of the Bulge. As they moved toward Bastogne, they had another near miss.

History in the Making

The conditions were miserably cold; few supplies were reaching them. Andy remembered breaking a chocolate bar into three—one section for each "meal" of the day. He also recalled seeing signs of the horrors of war. He kept his mind focused on the job. He was even able to sleep one night in a pigpen, just a few yards from where a 240-millimeter cannon fired on German positions. Each day rolled on to the next.

The retreat from Brest was a minor setback in comparison to the victory that would eventually come. In the meantime, there were miles to go and searches for a place to sleep.

"We were going through an area where all I recall is sleet, cold, mud, and rain. We came upon an empty house. We went in and noticed that there was a potbelly stove. Hoping we could get a fire going and warm up. Cleaning out the ashes, I looked down and found a little round coin. Why it was there, I don't know. I cleaned it off and found out it was an American three-cent piece, smaller than the dime. It was dated 1856."

Andy still has that coin to this day.

The US issued three-cent pieces similar to the one Sergeant Negra found.

A Simple, Special Christmas

Five months passed and the relentless cold intensified. Christmas in 1944 brought a special memory. "Christmas Eve of 1944, we stopped in Metz, France," said Andy. "We came to a halt, and all of a sudden, six trucks came at us. They were loaded with turkey, stuffing, and cranberry sauce for the whole Sixth Armored. We spent Christmas day in our vehicles, celebrating the birth of Christ."

Farther along, in Luxembourg, again trying to get out of the miserable conditions, they spent a night in a bowling alley. The following day, they arrived at the edge of Bastogne. At midnight, still inside the tank, they heard German voices. With a finger raised to his lips and a slow head shake, a sergeant indicated all the men needed to know.

Andy couldn't understand why he had again enjoyed such good fortune. The Germans never approached the tank. Andy suspected that they were scouts, not there to attack but to gain intelligence, where, as Andy recalled, they stayed for nearly a month. Andy's initial assignment was as a member of the survey section—he consulted maps and assisted in determining the location of German positions.

At the Battle of the Bulge, Andy was assigned to a role as tank gunner. He knew nothing about the tank or the gun, but he received instruction and advice. To avoid smashing his fingers while loading the large shells, he was told to ram them in with his fist. Following the Allied triumph at the Bulge, they continued to move across Europe, eventually totaling 1,500 miles on this tour of duty.

With over 200,000 combined casualties (killed, missing in action, wounded in action, and taken prisoner) on both sides, and with more than 1,400 civilians killed, the Battle of the Bulge was an epic and crucially important battle. Fought over one month, one week, and five days, it exacted a physical and mental toll on participants from both sides. The battle was the last offensive the Germans waged on the Western Front.

Along with the difficulties the weather presented, it was fought in a heavily forested area—the Ardennes region, bordering Belgium and Luxembourg. The Germans hoped to end the Allies' use of the port of Antwerp to disrupt supply lines. Divide-and-conquer was also the strategy the Germans employed. They hoped to drive a wedge and create a gap in the four Allied armies. They failed.

Things did not start out well for the Allies, but in time, despite being under-supplied and not being able to be reinforced by air because of the poor weather, they rallied. Even though they were outmanned, their lines spread too thin, and surrounded by German forces, the Allies pulled out a victory.

Analyzed by military experts and historians, and extensively covered in books and on screen, the Battle of the Bulge looms large in our collective past. It was also immortalized in episode six of Steven Spielberg's miniseries *Band of Brothers*. The Battle of the Bulge demonstrated that American courage, bound together with being on the side of the right, could enable American forces to overcome any challenge.

Andy's division eventually made it into Germany and helped liberate the Buchenwald concentration camp, near Weimar. Among the thousands of prisoners was Elie Wiesel, whose book *Night* continues to inspire and inform millions around the world. When the 6th Armored Division arrived at the place where 56,545 Jewish people were exterminated, Andy was profoundly heartsick at the extent of the inhumanity and atrocities of evil.

God as Guide

Andy recalled singing in the choir at the Russian Orthodox church, even though he didn't know what the Russian words he was singing meant, and remembered having a black shawl placed over his head in an Orthodox ceremony in which he confessed his sins. That led him to talk about prayer.

"I can't say that I prayed out loud much, if at all. But I always had the sense that God is inside me and guiding me and telling me what to do. He tells people where to go, how to treat other people, and how to accept people's criticisms of you. I know my place on this earth and how to live thanks to God."

Today, Andy still travels and speaks to groups. He wants to spread the message regarding what World War II meant for America and the rest of the world. The concentration camps were liberated, oppressed people were freed, and Hitler, Mussolini, and other horrific leaders and their reigns of terror were ended. He believes that as much as

America celebrates the Allied victory, other countries should as well. In Andy's estimation, had America failed in its mission, the world would be a very different place and likely even more fractured than it already is. He also sees his service as a reflection of the Great American Experiment.

"We were all strangers when we met. There were bankers. There were farmers. It was amazing how many of us came from different backgrounds and all of that. We weren't there to destroy and punish. We were there to help. I remember one time we were on the march, and we came across this farmer and his cow in Germany. She was struggling to give birth to a calf, and one of our guys, a first lieutenant, was an Iowa farm boy. He went over there to help the farmer and that cow. He spent forty-five minutes working to help that farmer out. They couldn't keep the calf alive, but that story just shows how Americans were willing to pitch in and do the right thing."

You'll Live Forever

Andy took a moment to reflect on his historic experience in a world war. Pausing thoughtfully, he said, "I remember how cold it was. I put all my socks and sweaters on. I remember taking helmet baths. You got yourself clean as best you could. There were a lot of difficult times for us. We got through them. We learned how to take care of ourselves. That's part of life: take care of yourself, keep a positive attitude, and you'll live forever."

*   *   *

Andy has traveled back to Normandy twice since the war and remains grateful for the kindness and appreciation shown to him and his fellow veterans by the French people. He has an immortal spirit. Youthful, energetic, and bursting with God's light, he leads by example, continuing to put service before self and showing gratitude above all else. Andy is the kind of man who immediately feels like family, both simultaneously impressive beyond measure and exuding a warmth that draws you in and welcomes you. A humble giant among us, Andy typifies the Greatest Generation, whose service we will remember forever.

A Life at Sea

My great-cousin Anton Lorenz enlisted as an apprentice seaman in the US Navy on August 20, 1923, and served over twenty-two years as a cook, a baker, and eventually chief commissary steward. His impressive career saw him serving on a variety of ships sailing far and wide, including the USS *Procyon*, flagship of the Pacific Fleet Supply Train; USS *Relief*, the hospital ship for the Pacific Fleet; USS *S-32*, a submarine; and the USS *Tutuila*, a river gunboat and a vital part of the Yangtze River Patrol (under the famed Lieutenant Commander S. E. Truesdell's command as captain). CCS Lorenz was stationed at Pearl Harbor, Hawaii, on the historic, deadly date of December 7, 1941.

Regular letters home to his family in Dayton, Ohio, convey the range of Anton's naval experiences and travel, from Christmas in the Philippines "Submarine Division Sixteen; Christmas and New Year's greetings from China and the Philippines 1928" (unlike modern submarines, the 'S' class subs had NO air-conditioning!) to exploring the Winter Palace in Peking "Dragon Wall in the Winter Palace. Had my picture taken in front of that." Documents issued at Hankow (now Wuhan), China, show Anton was transferred from the Asiatic Fleet out of Shanghai through Bremerton, Washington, en route to his next station in San Diego, California; just a few miles from where, seventy years later, his future great-cousin and his wife would fly jets for the same beloved Navy.

War!

In 1940, seventeen years into his service, Anton was stationed at Pearl Harbor, Hawaii. He lived with his family at Kaneohe Naval Air Station, a thirty-minute commute through the Koolau Mountain Range. They were all home during the early morning of Sunday, December 7, 1941.

Anton rushed to Pearl Harbor through the crush of chaos. He had to leave his wife and daughters behind, despite Kaneohe suffering extensive damage in the attack, too. Anton's daughter Geri shared her recollections of that awful day with my mother:

I was eight years old and my brother John was six. We lived on the base [Naval Air Station, Kaneohe Bay] in military housing very near the Marine guard gate. I remember

awakening early and looking out the bedroom window to watch what looked like planes far off in the distance engaged in bombing practice. I didn't think much about it again until my father and all military personnel were ordered to their duty stations. It then became apparent that the planes were not participating in bombing practice but were enemy aircraft.

Japanese Zeros flew over the houses (you could clearly see the rising sun on the underside of the wings) headed toward the airplane hangars to destroy the Navy planes still on the ground. I understand that they accomplished their mission.

Most everyone, I guess, was in a state of shock. I don't remember being fearful or aware of any panic at first. No homes were bombed or shot at; in fact, for a while we all stood outside to watch. Eventually, the reality of what was happening set in and we were told to get inside and put mattresses over the backs of the sofa and get under them. Later in the day, all families were told to leave the base and if possible stay with friends elsewhere on the island. Mother, John and I stayed with [friends] Paula, Dave and Alfred [Persson] for several days until we were able to return to the base. On that Sunday morning, Dave was in the hills hunting goats and when he heard the news, scooted on home and left the goats he had killed for mother and Paula to skin. At least we didn't go hungry while we were there.

Geri also shared her memories of the aftermath.

I don't remember how long it was before chaos returned to some sort of normalcy, but it must have been some time because mother tried to keep up our school work at home. When we did return to school, instead of fire drills we had bombing attack drills. We had to practice putting on gas masks, which we carried to school every day, and were marched outside into trenches which I guess were considered safer than being inside the building in case of an attack. We became familiar with the sound of the air raid siren while at home, and on one occasion I remember spending the night in a concrete bomb shelter. It was a false alarm; apparently someone thought a submarine was spotted near the island.

It is interesting looking back how we took all of this in stride. I guess it helped being eight. One of my favorite places to swim had been Kailua Beach. There were beautiful coconut groves along the beach, but after Pearl Harbor barbed wire was strung out along the shore and anti-aircraft guns strategically placed; it looked like a war zone. Blackouts were enforced and it was required that every house have black paper on all windows to keep light from showing outside. That Christmas when John and I awoke very early to see the presents under the tree, we had to use a flashlight with a special blue light to scope out which ones were ours.

That horrible surprise attack on American soil underscores that service members *and* their families were all interconnected in the defense of our country in some way. Service was not limited to the servicemember, and families shouldered burdens and sacrifice too.

This Associated Press news bulletin was transmitted over transpacific telephone that day.

WAR! OAHU BOMBED BY JAPANESE PLANES

Dec. 7. President Roosevelt announced this morning that Japanese planes had attacked Manila and Pearl Harbor.

"Attack Made on Island's Defense Areas. Oahu was attacked at 7:55 this morning by Japanese planes. The Rising Sun, emblem of Japan, was seen on plane wing tips. Wave after wave of bombers streamed through the clouded morning sky . . . the city was in an uproar. It is reliably reported that enemy objectives under attack were Wheeler field, Hickam field, Kaneohe bay and naval air station and Pearl Harbor.

CIVILIANS ORDERED OFF STREETS. The army has ordered that all civilians stay off the streets and highways and not use telephones . . . All navy personnel and civilian defense workers, with the exception of women, have been ordered to duty at Pearl Harbor. The Pearl Harbor highway was immediately a mass of racing cars. Thousands of telephone calls almost swamped the Mutual Telephone company . . . extra operators on duty.

All schools on Oahu, both public and private, will remain closed.

Home

In 1946, Anton retired from the Navy after twenty-two years of "faithful and honorable service." For the last eleven years of his life, he lived in warm Florida with his wife—with very special neighbors nearby: His cousin Luella Lorenz Cochran Davis and her husband, with whom they spent much time together. Anton died in 1991 at the age of 89. His ashes were scattered at sea, "placed to rest in the Gulf of Mexico at longitude 82° 52′ west and latitude 27° 43′ north," finally called Home after his lifetime voyage.

Nursing on the Front Lines

My great-great aunt, Lieutenant Luella Lorenz Cochran Davis, PFC Joseph Lorenz's sister and Anton Lorenz's cousin, joined the war effort in July 1943, alongside her husband, Frank, who joined the Merchant Marines. One world war after her brother was laid to rest in France and her brother-in-law shelled into a coma, Luella signed up for the US Army Nurse Corps the same month that saw Sicily invaded by the Allied Forces. Her years of service included a sixteen-month deployment throughout England, Germany, and France, where her primary duties were anesthesia and surgical nursing. She sent frequent letters home, which the family has faithfully kept as a deeply personal glimpse into the nursing front lines of World War II.

Following her discharge as a First Lieutenant, after the Allied Victory and her reunion with her husband and family, Luella returned to Fordham University under the G.I. Bill and obtained her Master of Social Sciences, continuing to work in hospitals in mental health social work. She called her whole career "practical Americanism." We call it valor.

Nurse, General Duty (3449)

On March 25, 1944, "Mrs. Luella B. L. Cochran" was appointed reserve nurse in the Army Nurse Corps and pronounced "Physically Qualified by The Surgeon." Luella departed for active duty six days later. As to the timing of her joining, she later wrote, "One would be prone to exclaim or question why I had waited for two years! However, only the younger nurses were asked for by the government [at first]."

Nurse anesthetists were in short supply in every theater of operations, so the Army developed a special training program for nurses in that specialty. More than two thousand nurses trained in a six-month course at Camp Maxey in Texas designed to teach them how to administer inhalation anesthesia, blood and blood derivatives, and oxygen therapy as well as how to recognize, prevent, and treat shock.

However, Luella did not have six months at Camp Maxey to complete such a training program; this might explain why she never received the official rating of anesthesia specialist, although those were the duties she performed during much of her service overseas. She served with the 125th Evacuation Hospital as Nurse, General Duty (3449).

Luella explained, "By spec number I mean that according to what you do, you have a number. For instance, mine might be 3449, which means I am a general duty nurse; the anesthetist's number may be 5436. Anyone looking at them would know immediately what our abilities are. I preferred to keep my old spec number instead of taking that of an anesthetist."

Off to War She Goes

By midnight of December 8, 1944, Luella and other members of the 125th Evacuation Hospital were aboard the British ship *Monarch* in New York Harbor, bound for Europe for what would eventually be a year and a half.

She wrote home often, and asked her family to save the letters; she intended to make a scrapbook with them all. Her first letter home let her mother know "Went to Communion last Sunday, yesterday and will go tomorrow. So don't worry. All is well. Have a very merry Xmas and Happy New Year. Much love to all of you."

Exactly one month later, Luella was assigned to temporary duty with the 121st Station Hospital in Braintree, England. "A station hospital is where the boys from the continent are first sent to here in England for care and disposition, which means either back to duty or to the States or limited service," she wrote home. Luella attended classes, studied, and gave anesthesia. Her first case was a leg amputation. In later years, she described her service duties:

Primary duties were anesthesia and surgical nursing. Was in charge of a surgical ward and contagion. Administered anesthetics to patients under the direction of a surgeon and advised the patients' condition and reaction to the anesthesia during operations. Immediately following anesthesia, maintained the equipment for anesthetic administration in serviceable condition.

Lipstick, Sardines, and American Officers

Lou's letters seldom described her actual daily duties, due to censorship and the need to protect wartime information. Yet what she did write was a delightful—and, at times, sobering—insight into the life of nurses in the war, including their interactions with American officers:

Am in the operating room now giving anesthesia. Like it a lot. I'm hoping that there will be a lot of mail waiting for me [at Tenby]. Am well and have a nice warm hut, sleeping between sheets, and get to occasional shows at the town on the tree. Went to a Red Cross sponsored dance last week and had only a fair time, for American officers are not all that the Act of Congress made them. As social beings they are of the high school caliber and very few h.s. boys can be called gentlemen in terms of sociability and the amenities of social behavior.

Am going to take a bath now, then go to the Officers Club. We undress in our huts, put on our robes, then take our torches (flashlights to you) and guide our way to the john and bath which roughly speaking is about a short block from home. Damp from a fresh bath we again find our way to our huts. I do believe that when I get home I'll be so used to inconveniences that I'll only be content with a pot-bellied stove and a fireplace and I'll have the bathroom at the other end of the lot in order to retain my memories. Ha.

I would appreciate it if you would send me: 3 pr. tan hose size #10; 1 box rochelle powder [an effervescing salt containing sodium bicarbonate and rochelle salt and tartaric acid, used as a cathartic or purgative]; 1 tube 'Joint Ease Mentholatum'; 1 Chen Yu (fairly dark) lip stick; sardines (small cans); box starch; cork screw; Creme shampoo; 2 pr rubber heels, brown; [this page is postmarked Dayton Ohio Parcel Post 16 April 1945; they had to show Lou's request in order to send a parcel overseas!].

Do keep well and thanks a lot for keeping the letters coming, All my love, Lou

The Basics

Luella's letters provided insights into civilian rationing occurring in Europe, and how difficult it was for some to obtain basic necessities—or how expensive certain "necessities" were!

1945 Feb 5, [121st Station Hospital, Braintree];

Dearest Mom and All;

I don't need any soap as I have enuf to last about two more months unless we go to France and I trade it in for something they have and I want. Soap is so scarce over there that the civilian gets for his week's ration, a bar about 3 inches long and 2 inches wide and half inch thick; so I'm told by the GI Joes.

I will make a list of some things I want at the end of the letter but will not mention scotch or rye or rum, but if you can send some it will be more than welcome. Soak off the label and mark it Shampoo with an S or Rm or Ri in the corner. We pay £3 15d for 15 Scotchs and 10 Gins or about a total of $14 or about 60¢ a drink and that is too much for little me.

A Brother in Arms Laid to Rest

While her letters purposely omitted war details, there were constant reminders of the destruction and death being suffered, and the relentless effort by the American and Allied troops. Luella began to wonder about the location of her brother Joseph's final resting place:

1945 Mar 28, Northern France; Dear Mom and All;

Today we marched to the little Catholic Church across the bridge which it is said we one time bombed, where memorial services were held for French and American soldiers. The padre then, still in his vestments, led the procession, the parishioners and us coming in the rear, up and up a mountainside until we were just about winded. He stopped at a little knoll that had been cleared and we all gathered in a semicircle around fifteen graves, all soldiers, thirteen French, one RAF and one Unknown. Requiem was sung, then a wreath laid, then the different people of the town laid bunches of spring blossoms on the graves. It was all very simple but impres-

Luella visiting her brother Anton's grave in Suresnes, France, in 1946.

Suresne Cemetery – Mar. 8, 1946

sive. There were tears in the eyes of many of the French women who were also dressed in black.

We were told today that we Americans had come in and rescued the town just in time to save a goodly number of Frenchmen whom the Germans were going to behead in front of the church. For this reason they hold no grudge against us for the damage we did here. Saw Laon [northeast of Soissons] and it is a shambles. Everything is peaceful here and I am in no danger so don't worry. I meant to ask you; where was Joe injured and where was he buried? I thot I might get a chance to visit it, if it was far enuf north; there may be some way to get to it. I seem so close and yet because I can't get to the cemetery; I feel so far away. Do keep well. All my love, Lou

Luella was able to visit Joseph's final resting place in the Suresnes American Cemetery twice while she was deployed, paying her respects and telling her little brother how deeply she missed him.

Got the Hell Out

Sometimes some details sneaked in. Her role was not without risk. Luella's hospital was moved behind the lines:

1945 Apr 12, Germany [left race track]; Dearest Mom and All;

Wrote you about two days ago and Frank last night. It is so difficult to write by candle light that I just about manage one letter a nite and try to alternate with Frank. Since here, we have made another move, more to the rear. Before we were just at the hinge of the pincer movement, which put us even ahead of the clearing station and between two barrages of fire. The danged things kept whizzing over our heads; first one side practiced firing the shells, then the other side played back. We got the hell out of that fire trap, as the saying in the Army goes.

A Christmas Gift for Every Soldier

Luella's letters show how the nurses endeavored to make holidays, especially Christmas, special for the troops: hosting parties, trimming the halls with decorations, and ensuring every single soldier received a gift. It's notable that Luella called them "boys"—such young men sacrificing so much. Luella wrote home on Christmas Day 1944, describing worship and celebration in wartime:

Dearest Mom and All;

Well, here it is Xmas Day. We've had a very nice one considering. Last night we met in the enlisted men's recreation hall with another unit and sang Xmas carols after which some of the male officers of our gang and some nurses went around to all the huts and serenaded them with carols. This morning we walked 3 miles to church. The ravages of war can be plainly seen in the neighborhood, also the scarcity of anything Christmasy did not allow them to be able to do any trimming and the church itself held only the crib and a few flow-

ers were on the altar. The priest had such a thick Welsh accent that unless we listened very attentively we could not understand him.

Our Xmas tree has been made by gathering limbs of holly and tucking them in a musette bag hung on the wall. We are giving the enlisted men a party tonight so we spent yesterday going through our foot lockers gathering sufficient gifts, even if it's ever so small, for each boy. Yesterday we nurses braved brambles, swamps and ditches to gather holly and mistletoe with which to trim their hall . . .

Love to all, Lou

Au Revoir . . . It's Time for the USO

Faith was important to those serving our country, and it was important to the Army to provide services for those who could attend. A year into Luella's service and after six months deployed (which entitled her to a "stripe on her sleeve"), she wrote home describing Sunday services:

Here we have them whenever and wherever we can. One Sunday in the Protestant chaplains and again for the last two Sundays, in the Officer's Mess tent. We have it any time of the day. You can consider yourself fortunate in this. One Sunday we had general absolution. Since then I've received Communion every Sunday. Does this make you feel good Mom? At least you know that I'm going to church regularly; I feel better about it too.

She went to describe the nightlife . . . and the continued saga between the nurses and the American officers:

Ruth is now powdering her nose for supper. Lea is too. And so we make ourselves beautiful. We like to let our officers see that we don't look dirty and faded all the time.

I'm here in Germany. Every day is the same now. We are still busy entertaining outside officers and ours just ogle from jealousy. But we've stopped trying to please them. They had their chance to escort us but muffed it. Now we are ignoring them. And let me tell you they don't like it. The shoe is on the other foot.

The wind was so strong last night it blew down our latrine. Can't you just picture that? It's turned chilly today and rainy. Regular monsoon weather. Hope it clears up by tomorrow . . .

We have our first USO show here tonight so must go now to get there in time. Au revoir and goodbye for now. Much love to all of you, Lou

*   *   *

Luella's letters provide exceptional insight into the realities of front line nursing in World War II. Nurses were not only vital to the medical care needed by injured troops, they were vital to their emotional well-being too. Competence during surgeries was just as important as a compassionate bedside manner and a nurturing care that helped soldiers feel not as far from home. From attending church services and spreading faith and encouragement, to providing holiday decorations and Christmas gifts, to attending USO shows and parties with the officers, nurses were the bright spot during wartime. As my mom says, "She was a spunky lady for sure!" A bright spot indeed.

Luella's cheerful letters also provide insight into the caliber of her character, strength of her faith, and dedicated service to others. Her irreplaceable descriptions are filled with the warmth of a nurse, but also that of a loving daughter, wife, and older sister. She sent most of her money home and never failed to keep up with family developments during her time abroad, always punctual with birthday and new baby greetings. Her family treasured her letters at the time, and we still do to this day.

*   *   *

On May 7, 1945, Germany signed an unconditional surrender at General Eisenhower's headquarters in Rheims, France; on May 8, President Truman announced the end of World War II in Europe (V-E Day, Victory in Europe); Czechoslovakia was liberated on May 9, and Russian troops occupied Prague on May 10. Luella's memoirs say "from 7 pm on May 7 to 7 am on May 8, Ruth and I had been in tent operating room. After the V-E announcement we folded up our tents and moved to St. Francis Hospital, run by nuns."

Luella proudly saved the order of the day dated May 10, 1945, announcing full victory in Europe by General Dwight D. Eisenhower. In the order, General Eisenhower described the service of the Americans and their allies, a fitting description for Andy, Anton, and Lou's service, in the name of freedom and for Good:

Your accomplishments at sea, in the air, on the ground and in the field of supply, have aston-

ished the world . . . Every man, every woman, of every nation here represented, has served according to his or her ability, and the efforts of each have contributed to the outcome. This we shall remember; and in doing so we shall be revering each honored grave, and be sending comfort to the loved ones of comrades who could not live to see this day.

Signed

DWIGHT D. EISENHOWER
HQ 15TH US ARMY; 10 MAY 1945

*Carry each other's burdens, and in this way
you will fulfill the law of Christ.*

—GALATIONS 6:2

The D-Day Prayer

On the night of June 6, 1944, President Franklin D. Roosevelt spoke to the nation via a radio broadcast. As the American war effort intensified, many had called for a Day of Prayer. Instead, the President charged Americans to pray every day, and led the nation in prayer together:

They will be sore tried, by night and by day, without rest—
until the victory is won. The darkness will be rent by noise and
flame. Men's souls will be shaken with the violences of war.

For these men are lately drawn from the ways of peace. They fight not for
the lust of conquest. They fight to end conquest. They fight to liberate. They
fight to let justice arise, and tolerance and good will among all Thy people.
They yearn but for the end of battle, for their return to the haven of home.

Some will never return. Embrace these, Father, and
receive them, Thy heroic servants, into Thy kingdom.

And for us at home—fathers, mothers, children, wives, sisters,
and brothers of brave men overseas—whose thoughts and prayers
are ever with them, help us, Almighty God, to rededicate ourselves
in renewed faith in Thee in this hour of great sacrifice.

Many people have urged that I call the Nation into a single day of special prayer.
But because the road is long and the desire is great, I ask that our people devote
themselves in a continuance of prayer. As we rise to each new day, and again when
each day is spent, let words of prayer be on our lips, invoking Thy help to our efforts.

Give us strength, too—strength in our daily tasks, to redouble the contributions
we make in the physical and the material support of our armed forces.

And let our hearts be stout, to wait out the long travail, to bear sorrows that may come, to impart our courage unto our sons wheresoever they may be.

And, O Lord, give us Faith. Give us Faith in Thee; Faith in our sons; Faith in each other; Faith in our united crusade. Let not the keenness of our spirit ever be dulled. Let not the impacts of temporary events, of temporal matters of but fleeting moment let not these deter us in our unconquerable purpose.

With Thy blessing, we shall prevail over the unholy forces of our enemy. Help us to conquer the apostles of greed and racial arrogancies. Lead us to the saving of our country, and with our sister Nations into a world unity that will spell a sure peace, a peace invulnerable to the schemings of unworthy men. And a peace that will let all men live in freedom, reaping the just rewards of their honest toil.

Thy will be done, Almighty God.

PART III

The War Comes Home

Luella's portrait from 1944. At one point, nine of her
family members were serving in the war.

Luella in Bad Kreuznach, Germany, 1945.

A proud member of
the 82nd Airborne,
Sergeant Michael Verardo
in Afghanistan, 2010.

Sarah with her husband,
Mike, and their children
on his "Alive Day."

13

If It's Not Good, God's Not Done

Sarah Verardo,
Founder, Save Our
Allies; CEO, The
Independence Fund

Sergeant Michael
Verardo, US Army
(Retired)

Sarah Verardo has known her husband almost her whole life—all the way back to being childhood friends at age fourteen. They were at their small school together just a few hours north of New York City during the horrific terror attack on 9/11, after which Mike and his friends resolved to defend and serve this country by enlisting in the US Army.

Mike needed a few painful surgeries even to medically qualify to enlist, and Sarah supported him during that recovery. She stood proudly by his side on one of the best days of his life, when he received his coveted 82nd Airborne patch. And she covered him in prayer when he was able to take the fight to the enemy, deploying to Afghanistan in 2009.

Then, just fourteen days apart in April 2010, Mike was hit by two IEDs. The first was very serious and required a medevac; in the second, a catastrophic explosion blew off his left leg and most of his left arm and burned over 30 percent of his body. Mike was radioed in, expected dead on arrival; although he flatlined several times during the medevac, when they landed he miraculously had a pulse.

Sarah has been there by his side every day since, throughout years in the hospital and years on a recovery path that included over one hundred surgeries for his polytraumatic conditions. She learned how to pack his wounds, serving as caretaker in the US Department of Veterans Affairs' void, saying goodbye to her husband over and over, and living the realities of how severe injuries, both seen and unseen, can progress far beyond a date someone "survived," or as Sarah calls it, Mike's Alive Day.

And through it all, Sarah is raising three phenomenal, faith-filled daughters whose memories of their father are different than their present-day experiences, who have in their mother a model of what loving the Lord and loving your husband unconditionally look like.

The "front line" can take many forms.

Purple Hearts

Before Michael deployed to Afghanistan with the 82nd Airborne Division, Sarah held a typical binary approach to the risks of combat. She thought her love was either going to war and coming home, or going to war and not coming home. "But," she told me, "no one had ever talked about this middle ground that our wounded live in for the entirety of their lives in some cases."

Mike was severely injured by two different IEDs, on two different dates, and received two Purple Hearts. "The first time he was hit was April 10, 2010," Sarah said. "He was riding in a truck as the gunner. They hit a roadside IED, and the blast was so powerful the turret he was in twisted in the air thirty feet. They medevaced him out. After they evaluated him, they gave him the choice of going back to the United States to heal or going back with his unit. Family and friends would have preferred that he come on home."

Mike's unit, 2nd Battalion, 508th Parachute Infantry Regiment, 82nd Airborne, was taking heavy casualties. Twenty-four men were sent home and 65 percent of his unit received a Purple Heart. By the spring of 2010, more than one thousand American troops had been killed in Afghanistan while taking on the Taliban. Mike's deployment was part of a larger surge in numbers sent there. Still, with the same resolve Mike displayed in enduring those surgeries to enlist, he stayed. He wasn't going to go home and leave his brothers behind.

While Mike was recovering in Kandahar, two of his very good friends were hit with an IED. Specialist Joey Caron was killed. Mike took his hand and put it on Joey's coffin. Then he made another pact: *I'm going back out to the fight.*

"And he went back out," Sarah said. "And on his very first foot patrol back in action it was just game over. He was the eighth guy and they're taking a wall. And it was an old Russian land mine that the Taliban had hooked up to fifteen-gallon jugs of homemade high explosives. The IED went off and the force of the blast blew off his left leg and much of his left arm. He was burned about thirty percent of his body. He was dragged to casualty collection burned and maimed. His medevac was called in.

"When they radio for a medevac, the wounded are assigned a classification: seriously injured, not seriously injured. Michael was called in as very seriously injured, expected dead on arrival. And the first hurdle that he jumped over was flatlining several times while still in the air. Fortunately, he still had a pulse when he landed. And that was just the beginning of this very, very, very long journey that we continue to be in fourteen years later."

A Foundation of Faith

Before Michael gave Sarah an engagement ring, he gave her a Bible. "He said to me that the most important thing we need to do for each other is focus on our holiness and not our happiness," Sarah said. "To get each other to heaven. Faith was something that was always a part of my life. The real test of faith is when things are not going well or when you can't make sense of what is happening. At those difficult times, I understand that things will be okay because with God, if it's not good, He's not done."

The IED attack in 2010 left Mike with polytraumatic conditions that have required more than one hundred surgeries. Along with that, he has spent years in speech, visual, physical, and occupational therapy. Despite all his trauma, Mike still wanted to keep serving.

As Sarah told me, "Mike really wanted to continue on active duty. He loved being a paratrooper. He wanted to jump again. He was so determined. And I'll never forget the day that the Army's med board came back and said that he could not effectively evade live fire. He was just devastated.

"I realized that day that he wasn't doing as well as we had hoped. I needed to step in and relieve him of duty almost—and tell him that I've got this. I will help us navigate the big question that faces a lot of veterans—*what are you going to do next?*

"Mike had essentially been in the hospital for three years. During that time, I would find myself walking the halls and talking to God about how much more could Mike take. Seeing someone you love in that kind of pain and enduring surgery after surgery. He'd have to go under anesthesia every twenty-four hours so that they could change the bandages on his burns. It was such a horrific process.

"Every time, for years, he['d] come out of anesthesia and wake up believing that he was back in Afghanistan. He'd scream for his medic. I thought that this was an untenable situation, for him to have to relive that horrible experience over and over. It wasn't just the physical pain he was enduring; it was the emotional pain that had to be so debilitating."

We know that all things work for the good of those who love God, who are called according to His purpose.

—ROMANS 8:28

"That's when I had to tell myself that God is not done. There is a point and a plan to all this. I've always loved Romans, and I really do believe that God is knitting all these incidents and events together for the greater good. What that will look like, I don't know. But I have to trust right now."

The Strength to Kneel

Mike and Sarah moved to Rhode Island in 2013 so that Mike could continue his recuperation. There Mike went to Mass every day. Even when he couldn't walk, he still found the strength to kneel during the service.

"I think that he had to make sense of everything that happened to him, not just the IED and what it did," Sarah said. "He had to deal with not being able to return to duty, with being plucked from the brothers that he loved and having no satisfying conclusion to his military career. We'd find peace, and then something would happen that left us feeling like the rug got pulled out from under us again."

For Mike and Sarah, one of the most difficult aspects of his injuries was being able to get him the proper care that he needed. The bureaucratic, underequipped Department of Veterans Affairs (VA) presented them with additional challenges. Despite being catastrophically injured, it was difficult for Mike to get appointments to see the medical and rehabilitative specialists he so badly needed. Sarah resorted to YouTube videos to learn how to pack Mike's open wounds herself. When Mike's prosthetic leg broke, she had to duct-tape it together and wait for a replacement.

That situation prompted a move to North Carolina later in 2013, hoping the VA care there was more dependable. And they got married.

"Despite how much medical uncertainty we faced, we were so happy. I remember turning to one of my girlfriends—her husband had also been wounded—and her agreeing with me that we were the lucky ones. These two men are *alive*. We were so fortunate. And Mike and I felt like that for so many years. We were truly living on hope. God had granted Michael a second chance. We had some really rough days, but we also knew that there was this plan."

Surviving Survival

"I didn't realize that survival wouldn't be a period at the end of that sentence, but rather a continuation that would change day to day, year to year in ways that sometimes felt like a nightmare to me," Sarah said. "In 2017, I was pregnant with our third daughter. I began to notice some things with Mike that I hadn't before. We were so focused on his physical health that it took a while for me to realize that he could no longer tell his left from his right."

Neuropsychological evaluations revealed that the traumatic brain injury he suffered in that blast was more serious than they'd previously known. There were additional questions: Was this the result of that initial injury or were the effects of all the anesthesia he'd been administered a contributing cause?

On April 24, 2019, "As Mike was being wheeled into surgery, I thought about how nine years ago to that day, he was on that medevac flight clinging to life," Sarah said. "Now, here we are, nine years later, and Mike has to undergo a twelve-hour surgery. He survived it but his recovery was horrible. This one was really scary. At one point, a doctor told me he thought it was a good idea that I go home and get my kids and bring them to see their dad one last time.

"All I could think of was how young they were, how little they were. I didn't know how to tell them that Dad's not going to win this fight. For so long, to explain his injuries, I'd told them about what Dad had done. He'd gone somewhere to fight the bad guys and he won. Then I wondered if I was supposed to tell them that he didn't win this time. I couldn't even make sense of it. I was absolutely distraught.

"I went out of his hospital room and I got on my knees and I must have said to myself two hundred times, *Blessed is she who has believed that the Lord fulfills His promises to her*. And I felt this overwhelming sense of peace, that God had us. Whatever happened,

I knew was supposed to happen. I also knew that Michael had a personal relationship with Jesus, and that it was going to be okay. God wasn't done, and it wasn't good to me. But I also realized that what is good to me, may not be good to him."

Michael spent another year in the hospital and returned home late in 2019. Though he was home, he still needed to be in a hospital bed and he required twenty-four-hour-a-day nursing care.

"That's when it hit me that I was yet again going to have to grieve another version of my husband," Sarah said. "He was no longer able to fully function as my husband. Obviously, that was devastating. As the years have gone by, I feel like I've lost more and more of him. But being able to see parts of him through my girls, like some of the facial expressions they make, or the things they say, and I just think *you are your dad*. That's wild, and just such a blessing."

Sacred Ground

In October 2019, Michael had a heart attack. Once again, Sarah thought that she was going to lose Michael. Once again, he pulled through. Since then, his neurological function has continued to deteriorate and his physical state will always be tenuous. Still, the two of them press on and rise to every challenge.

When the Taliban took over the capital city of Kabul in August 2021, overthrowing the Islamic Republic of Afghanistan's government and replacing it with their own, Sarah knew that this news would be difficult for Michael to hear. She knew that only she could be the one to tell Michael.

"He doesn't process things through conversation the way he used to. He understands things, but there isn't the same kind of back-and-forth. And this was one of the worst days of my life having to tell him about Afghanistan. He didn't really say much to me. He has his dog, Bravo, named after his beloved Bravo Company. He hugged Bravo and looked at me and nodded. I left the room. A moment later I heard him wailing. I went back in and I could see how distraught he was. He told me that he wished he wasn't like he was. He wanted to go and help those people.

"I decided that this was one more thing that I wanted to take on for him. I knew how important Afghanistan was to him. That place was holy ground to him. So many men that he loved took their last breaths there. How could we not treat it like sacred ground?"

Sarah with the president of Afghanistan.

In 2015, Sarah allied herself with the Afghan government. She was hoping to find a way to recognize and honor the efforts that Michael and other veterans made during Operation Enduring Freedom, to celebrate the contributions made by both American troops and their Afghan partners. Save Our Allies, dedicated to rescuing and serving Americans and Allies in war-torn environments, is the outgrowth of her work.

She didn't stop there. A suicide prevention program she created has saved thousands of lives. The Independence Fund is a nonprofit that has changed the lives of countless catastrophically wounded veterans and their families. As a result of her work and Mike's sacrifices, she has garnered nationwide support for her endeavors, including from former President Donald J. Trump and former Secretary of Defense James N. Mattis, both of whom formally supported her efforts to come to the aid of veterans and their caretakers.

I Know Jesus

"Now it feels as if there's no reciprocity in our relationship, and that's okay," Sarah told me. "It's very hard. But it's also made easier because it is exactly what God wants us to do. It's okay because that is how God loves us. I honor Him by honoring my husband. I understand that our relationship now is kind of unconditional, one-way. Because of Michael's condition, he's taught my girls about unconditional love. He's shown them that sometimes you love someone who can't return that love without any expectations. With Michael and I, we've entered into a sacrificial love. I feel like every day God hits this reset button for me and I get the message that *I can do this*. I'm called to do it. And the truth is, I'm not doing it alone. That's the great part because Jesus Christ is with me all day, every single day.

"I miss Mike every day. I thought that the two of us were going to have so much time together. I have had to say goodbye to him so many times, in so many different ways. And on some of those nights, I've crawled into bed and I feel covered in the Holy Spirit. I truly do. I feel as though God is telling me, it may not be okay right now, but it will be okay. This is part of a bigger picture and plan. And of all the things I try to do, the most important is to point my children to the Lord and have them trust Him like I do—with all my heart, all the time, no matter what.

"To me, this is the incredible power of prayer. We thought Mike wasn't going to be able to walk again. He did. He was able to survive surgeries and serious blood loss, he's come out of medically induced comas, he's bounced back from strokes, and all of these things just should not have been possible. I feel the presence of a huge population of people, God's warriors, who are always caring, always praying, always cheering for us and just making us feel so loved. And those warriors for Christ—I'm so grateful, so blessed."

A few years ago, Mike was in the hospital again. After the procedure, he was neither verbal nor mobile for forty-eight hours. She stood at his bedside asking the doctors, "What's going to happen? What if he dies?"

Then Mike spoke for the first time in two days: "I'm not afraid of that. I know Jesus."

"And then I just thought," said Sarah, "again, it is all—no matter what—going to be okay."

*   *   *

Sarah and her warrior husband grew their family on a bedrock foundation of impenetrable faith, of love for Jesus Christ. This family is on the front lines of what surviving postcombat polytraumatic conditions looks like. Every day, Sarah's prayers are answered: their three girls love Jesus and love their mom and dad, in a joyful home filled with faith and hope.

And it is never without purpose. "Because of Michael, a lot of people, a lot of Afghans in particular, have benefited because of what he has gone through. His interpreter, Johnny, has four little girls living a mile from us in America. If it wasn't for Michael Verardo, that would have never happened."

Sarah is a walking angel among us. Her strength, love, and godliness are humbling to witness, and it's an honor to witness the way she loves her husband. Running two not-for-profit organizations, all while raising three young girls and caring for a husband with enormous needs, is a colossal earthly lift. Her faith in God's plan, her love for Him, and His unconditional love for her allows her to take on more than most people could bear.

Blessed is she who believes that the Lord will fulfill

His promises to her!

—LUKE 1:45

US Marines praying over
a fallen brother in
Fallujah, Iraq, in 2004.

Sergeant Gabriel De Roo in Iraq in 2006.

14

Gabriel's Light

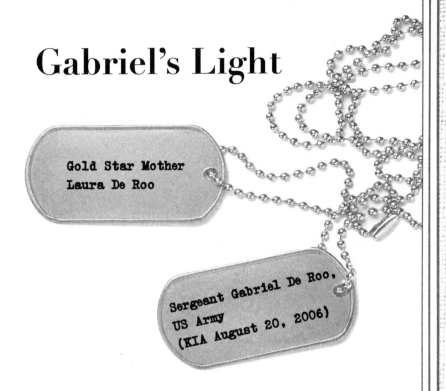

Gold Star Mother
Laura De Roo

Sergeant Gabriel De Roo,
US Army
(KIA August 20, 2006)

Gabriel De Roo enlisted in the US Army at the age of twenty-one, covered in prayer by his Christ-centered family. Sergeant De Roo was a dedicated soldier and a dedicated Christian. Nicknamed "John 3:16" by his fellow soldiers, he unfailingly proved his commitment to his biblical values, like once undergoing dozens of extra push-ups after refusing a drill sergeant's order to swear. More importantly, Gabriel knew the importance of knowing Jesus in our lifetime. He told his parents Laura and David, "If there's a grenade, I'm going to be the first one on it. These other guys need more time to get right with God."

In between Sergeant De Roo's two deployments to Iraq, he welcomed the birth of his son, Gabriel De Roo II. Six months later, he deployed for the second time to Iraq. He loved writing letters to his family and sending care packages and surprises to his wife, Hannah, while he was deployed. One of his letters to his parents included this quote from John Stuart Mill:

War is an ugly thing, but not the ugliest of things. The decay and degraded state of mind that thinks nothing is worth fighting for is far worse.

On August 20, 2006, Sergeant De Roo was killed by a sniper's bullet. The day after his wife was notified of his death, a care package arrived for her: flowers, chocolate, and a loving note from Gabriel. In the words of the church where his memorial was held, "It was as if sent from heaven."

One of his postcards home to Laura and David read, "Please pray for us . . . that we would be godly parents who will teach little Gabriel to love God. I can never thank you enough for raising me with a firm foundation in the Scriptures."

This is Laura's story.

A Lighthouse

The De Roo family was a strong Christian household that served the Lord. "Faith was the predominant part of our home, wanting to please the Lord in what we did and how we did it," Laura shared with me. The De Roos attended church on Sundays and involved their children in additional youth church programs, homeschooling them until high school to ensure that their academic studies were incorporated with their faith teachings. They regularly corresponded with missionaries around the world, and prayer and scripture were fundamental to their peace-filled days. "Our beliefs were a complete part of our lives," Laura said.

I've had the privilege of going on missionary trips to Uganda, Zambia, and Malawi, as well as here in the United States. I treasured being part of missions, part of an endeavoring lighthouse that helps to spread faith and healing. As Gabriel grew up, he served as a lighthouse, spreading faith and modeling a committed Christian existence.

Laura noticed Gabriel's faith deepening and his focus sharpening as he grew into a young man, beginning in high school and growing even stronger after he enlisted in the Army. During Gabriel's first deployment in 2004, he was in contact with a young woman named Hannah, whom he met shortly before leaving. They married that same year, and Hannah gave birth to Gabriel Glen De Roo II in December 2005. Gabriel's wife, her preacher father, and his brothers-in-law all sharpened each other's iron. Gabriel attended Bible study and participated in prayer groups. Strong in faith before this, his rock-solid foundation strengthened further as he dug deeper.

In one of his letters home, Gabriel wrote that he was praying that he was a godly example to all those around him, and that he would give 100 percent. The effort to dedicate himself to his Army duties was one thing; to be a great example as a Christian was another. "For Gabriel, it was a tug-of-war," Laura explained. "He did have a strong desire to represent Christ in a field that desperately needed it. He knew that his teammates weren't ready to die, were not ready to meet God. So, even when his time came, he didn't have the opportunity to make that choice. I think he would have been glad to do it if he had. Having a walk with the Lord is such a core part of who he was as an individual; he was amazing."

Though finding those who were truly receptive to God's word might have been a challenge, it was clear that Gabriel's teammates were paying attention to the example he set. They called him John 3:16: "*For God so loved the world, that he gave His only Son, that whoever believes in Him should not perish but have eternal life.*" We spoke about the extra push-ups Gabriel underwent, and Laura was proud of—and not surprised by—his steadfast commitment. "Knowing that Gabriel endured that means a lot. I'm not surprised he made that choice. He truly wanted to be an example to those he served with. He was willing to do whatever he had to do to keep his faith strong."

A Present and a Future in Christ

Gabriel realized his role in the Army gave him an opportunity to do more of God's work. While deployed, he wrote home about his sense of purpose in healing the Iraqi people and expressed a desire to return to Iraq to minister after the war. He shared about fellowship and Bible studies he led there, and seizing opportunities to share God's Word with so many of his fellow soldiers.

Hannah met Gabriel while he was stationed at Fort Lewis in Washington State. She was his pastor's daughter; Hannah's father ministered to Gabriel about the risks of being in combat. He also spoke of hope and purpose. Life was like a jigsaw puzzle, Hannah's father told him, and God was actively moving and connecting pieces. The two of them had been connected by God, part of a larger picture to be assembled. Whether or not he returned from Iraq, God was the sovereign Father with the entire picture in His hands.

09 MAR 03

DeRoe Family,

I'm glad I had the chance to talk to most of
you today; it's encouraging to hear your voices.
It has been a good day (relaxing almost) today. We
woke up at 5 a.m. and cleaned the barracks before
formation. (After breakfast (chow) we had Bible study.
The Chaplin (sp) updated us on some current events and
sports scores before we talked about finding God's will.
Kentucky's pretty good this year, huh!? After that we marched
to the chapel down the road. The chapel services are
good, but not great. I enjoy singing the old hymns and
some of the newer ones like: "Awesome God", Lord we lift Your
Name on High, and "Power of Your Love". After the service
I finished P.J.'s letter and wrote a quick one to Grandpa
and Grandma. Nine of us attended the Protestant service
this morning and we're talked about finding some time during
the week to start our own Bible study. Pray that I
live as a Godly example to those around me and that I
give 100% all the time.

I was assigned to Battalion staff duty with another guy
Thursday night and I had a chance to read some facts
about Ft Benning. One was that General Patton's Headquarters
were in a building that is a 1/2 mile from our barracks.
If you hear any more updates on the Middle East by the
time you get this, let me know. Dad, it looks like the
Tigers have a good shot at the pennant (sp) this year. Mom, thank
you for the phone card, it is greatly appreciated. How is your
business going?

(the messages are well)

(answer the phone & it rings)

• Send a family picture or two if you have a chance.

Chasidy and Chastity, how is school going? What are your plans for the summer? Angel, what's new in GA? I don't know if I told you guys this, I have a Drill Sergeant from Grand Rapids. Are you getting along with your roomate okay? P.J., let me know how track is going. I hope things are going well for all of you. I'll write more when I can. I should have an opportunity to call again this weekend. Below is a couple of quotes I've seen that I think are pretty good and ones that I believe in.

Until later,
Your son and brother,
Gabriel

" To be prepared for war is one of the most effectual means of preserving the peace."
    - Pres. George Washington

" War is an ugly thing, but not the ugliest of things. The decayed and degraded state of mind that thinks nothing is worth fighting for is far worse."

    - John Stuart Mill

" Encourage us in our endeavor to live above the common level of life. Help us to choose the harder right instead of the easier wrong."

    - West Point Cadet Prayer

Devoted son, brother, and Christian, Gabriel De Roo writes home to his family during deployment.

Gabriel's Light

Gabriel made the Ultimate Sacrifice on August 20, 2006, during his second deployment. His son was eight months old. Gabriel's life, and the loss, had a profound impact on so many. "God guided him in his growth, so that his life would make that much of a difference," Laura shared. "And I think my life hasn't been the same since we lost Gabriel. I wouldn't have the context to help myself or others with the things we all face had it not been for the loss. If it hadn't been for Gabriel and my loss, I wouldn't have gone in the direction that God has allowed me to go."

After Gabriel was killed, Laura helped start a local chapter of Blue Star Mothers of America. Nearly six thousand members strong, the organization is "mothers, stepmothers, grandmothers, foster mothers and female legal guardians who have children serving in the military, guard or reserves, or children who are veterans. We support each other and our children while promoting patriotism. Our organization focuses on our mission every single day and will never, ever forsake our troops, our veterans or the families of our Fallen Heroes."

Laura saw that other mothers in the area had children who were in the battleground. She saw that their strength was low and their fears were great, and they had no one to share those fears with. She felt God's urging to do so, and it became a very important part of her life.

"It still is," she said. "God gave me the opportunity to speak, to share my faith, to share Gabriel's story. It has also helped knowing what Gabriel was doing, how much it meant to him, and the commitment that he had. How can you be indifferent? God has upheld us, encouraged us, and kept us going."

Laura's efforts on behalf of families of the fallen grew. In 2011, she started a local American Gold Star Mothers (AGSM) chapter. The mission of these mothers is "working together to honor and preserve the memory of our fallen children by continuing their service to the military community." The loss these families suffer leaves an unfathomable void. Gold Star families become an extended family, united in their shared experience, their grief, and the honor of the fallen's legacy.

Since 2019, Laura has served as the AGSM Department of Michigan president. In this role, she has had lots of opportunities to share Gabriel's story. Laura sees this as a divine gift in the wake of her loss. "God has been faithful to allow me to do this. He has opened many doors that I would never have walked through if it weren't for Gabriel's loss."

Among the duties Laura has taken on as department president is to present Gold Star banners for the families after their loss. She considered it a privilege, but at the funerals of the fallen, she noticed another void. God and Jesus were seldom mentioned in the official services. Fear of offense took precedence over an open expression of faith.

"I would see over and over again the military person conducting the service would talk about a 'higher power,'" Laura said. "They never talked about Jesus Christ, never talked about God. They used terms that weren't going to offend anyone's sensibility or idea of who's in charge of the world. I feel that creates a great emptiness in the military."

"Maybe that's why Gabriel's light shone so brightly," Laura added. "Because there was this darkness."

An Eternal Impact

And now Laura is able to spread the gospel in Gabriel's name, just as he did in his life. "It is hard to not have him here with us now. We miss him terribly. But to know that his story can be used to further the gospel and to share Jesus Christ with others, I think that Gabriel would be very pleased to know that's his legacy." Laura's faith has sustained her throughout the loss of her only son, and she knows firsthand the strength it can provide Gold Star families. "I don't know how many parents suffer the loss that we've suffered and not have the Lord in their life to sustain them." Now, many more do, thanks to Laura and her efforts.

It is incredibly rewarding for Laura to know the impact Gabriel had in his life sharing Jesus with so many. "Gabriel's witness was so bright in the time he was here," Laura reflected. "Especially the last few years that he was in the military when his life was different. Because it *was* so different. He stood out. That's pretty exciting in itself, to be able to say that your child learned that much from home, but also on his own. That doesn't mean I wouldn't rather have him here. But it's pretty amazing to be able to walk with the Lord Jesus and have Him in your life." And the impact Gabriel has had will last far longer than his life: "His impact was an eternal type of impact, because he got people to commit their lives to the Lord."

*   *   *

Gabriel led a life of distinction by example: a strong Christian man who loved the Lord with all his might and who loved his fellow man almost as much. The impact Gabriel had in his short life is greater than most who lead full lifetimes; he was a special soul who inspired everyone around him to be better, to serve Christ and each other, irrespective of wartime boundaries and lines drawn in the sand.

His fellow warriors were blessed for it, and there is no one prouder of it than his Gold Star mother. Laura raised Gabriel in a house serving the Lord, and watched with gratification as he grew into a faith-filled man, husband, and soldier. He in turn inspired her; she now spreads the gospel in his name, sharing Gabriel's story, his sacrifice, and his light for all to see.

Blessed are those who hunger and thirst for righteousness,
for they shall be filled.

—MATTHEW 5:6

Sergeant Gabriel De Roo posing with his family
before his graduation from boot camp. From left are his
sister Patience; Gabriel; his mother, Laura; and his sisters
Charity and Angel in 2003.

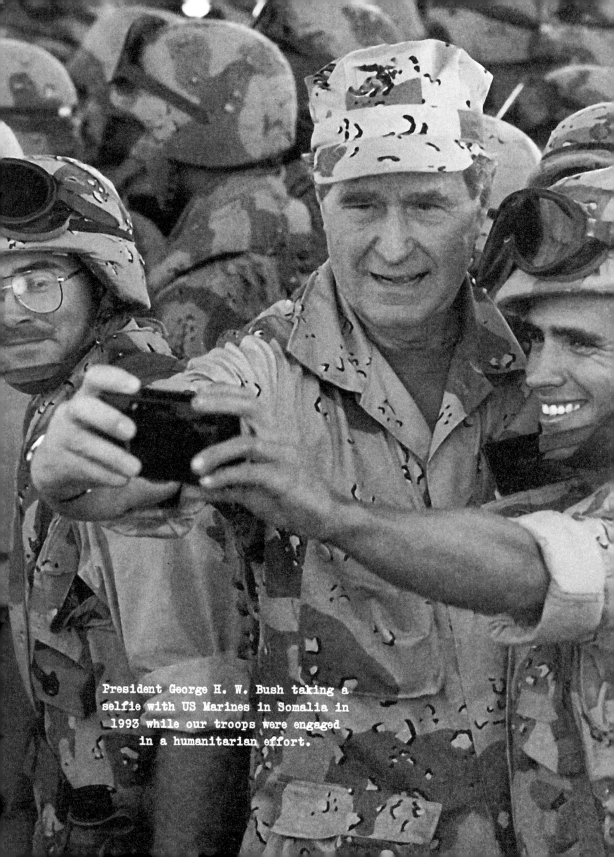

President George H. W. Bush taking a selfie with US Marines in Somalia in 1993 while our troops were engaged in a humanitarian effort.

Tom and Jen Satterly, the cofounders of the
All Secure Foundation, which is dedicated to assisting
our special operations warfighters.

15

All Secure

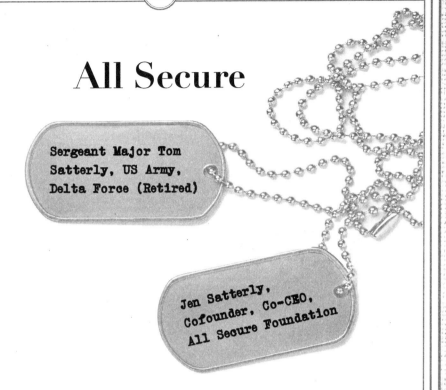

Sergeant Major Tom
Satterly, US Army,
Delta Force (Retired)

Jen Satterly,
Cofounder, Co-CEO,
All Secure Foundation

Command Sergeant Major Tom Satterly, US Army, Delta Force special operator, was as elite a warfighter as they come. Tom's first combat mission was the historic Battle of Mogadishu in Somalia in 1993. The remainder of Tom's highly decorated career was hallmarked by elite missions—many headline-making, like the capture of Saddam Hussein—and hundreds of covert operations in the shadows, preserving and protecting freedom away from the limelight.

Tom met the love of his life after retiring from the Army: Jen, an esteemed contractor with special operators. They were a perfect match, sharing professional and personal passions, both incredibly accomplished and driven by purpose. It would seem the hardest part was over, only peace ahead, the risks to Tom's life extinguished.

But the reality was—as it is for so many of our combat veterans—that the biggest fight, the hardest fight, was yet to come. That fight would see Tom once a month holding a gun to his head, begging Jen to allow him to take his life.

The enemies and demons our warfighters face are not always left on the physical battlefield.

The Need for the All Secure Foundation

Jen and Tom founded the All Secure Foundation in 2017 to help special operator warriors and their families heal from the trauma of war. Jen and Tom and their team assist special operations active-duty and combat veterans and their families in recovery from PTS through education, awareness, resources for healing, marriage retreats, and PTS resiliency training. "All secure" is the call that goes out over the radio during a combat mission to signal that everyone is accounted for and that everything is okay, that the target is secure and threats have been eliminated. Their nonprofit has served thousands of families, helping to heal internal wounds with very real biological symptoms, addressing the body, mind, and spirit in turn.

During Jen's years as a special operations embed, she began to see a pattern with the elite warriors she was working alongside—the same pattern being revealed in her husband. Symptoms these men displayed included anger issues, anxiety, severe depression, isolation, and a long list of medical challenges. These warfighters she was surrounded by, and her combat veteran husband, were all suffering from complex post-traumatic stress.

The Road to Restoring Faith

Jen made it her mission to help not only the warfighters but also their families, who often suffer from secondary PTS and are innocent casualties of combat. She became a certified health and wellness coach to better understand the biology of PTS. Her husband joined the effort, and they cofounded All Secure. They believe it is Tom's most important mission to date. In their relentless effort to completely heal these warfighters, they realized how fundamental the spirit component was. Treatments and therapies can address the body and the mind, but true healing cannot exist without restoring the spirit. And this only comes with restoring faith.

While Jen was working with these warfighters, she marveled at their courage and bravery. But she began to notice a troubling trend. "One Ranger told me, 'I'm going to hell anyway. So, it doesn't really matter what I do the whole rest of my life.' He was maybe twenty-six years old. And I said, 'Why do you think you're going to hell?' He told me that he was raised by a minister father in Kentucky, and he can't even go home. He can't look his father in the face. He killed too many people. His father always told him to turn the other cheek. So, he now 'knows' I'm going to hell."

The young warrior's views were distressing. Was this the burden he was carrying—that if he didn't turn the other cheek he was going to be rejected by family and God? That doing his duty in war would result in everlasting suffering? Jen asked the operators if this was a common theme. It was. She learned there were so many warfighters who had been very spiritual or very religious, but then in the hell of war had lost their faith, lost their way, and demonized themselves.

Jen told me there is a complex issue of our warriors bumping against the "Thou shalt not kill" commandment. "We had an amazing chaplain, who sat down with Tom eight years ago and told him you're reading it all wrong. It's not 'Thou shalt not kill'; it's 'Thou shalt not *murder*,'" she said.

Moreover, war is a big part of the Bible. "It's full of God saying take this tribe out or take that tribe out," Jen said. "From King David and on down, you look at all of these warfighters and all of these amazing leaders of the early church, and the acts of violence they had to commit." There is also a persistent theme of forgiveness, no matter how terrible one's acts might have been. "Look at Saul, who became Paul, how he used to kill Christians for fun. Then he becomes one of the leaders of and the founders of our church," Jen said. "There's so much forgiveness in the Bible, there's so many stories of the screwed-up individual who did some really messed-up stuff. And look how God favored that person."

None of this helps if our warfighters aren't getting that story. The reality is, they're getting—and internalizing—a very different one. "When I started seeing these young men lose their faith, lose their hope, it was no surprise to me that the suicide rate is what it is, because there's a real lack of God," Jen said. "In war, there's a real lack of love, of compassion, empathy; there's not very much space for it." Her husband had been wrestling with that issue before their talk with the chaplain as well. "And we know that God knows individuals' hearts. I know He knew Tom's; He knew mine. But Tom and I were struggling."

Jen Becoming Whole

Jen had been carrying a negative association with religion, stemming from childhood abuse. "Eventually, the religious part of me met the rebellious part of me," she said. She came to realize part of her rebellion was a result of her own post-traumatic stress. "I was raised in a very abusive household. Religion was tied to that abuse as well," she explained. "I walked away from my faith in my early twenties. I still believed in God and Jesus but

I was not a faithful follower. It was easier to make bad decisions as a nonbeliever but my life was actually so much harder without Christ. I was floundering. At times I felt like I was in a living hell." Jen spent almost fifteen years searching for answers.

Then she accepted Him back in her life. "Once I surrendered and said, 'I'm born again, and this is my new life,' everything started changing—including my healing. Now, when people ask if I feel like I have PTS, no, I don't. I'm healed. That box is checked, and it would never have been sanctified if I didn't find Jesus. Without his healing, I would still be incomplete."

Jen realized firsthand that the spiritual component, the need for faith, was just as important as healing physical injuries. That a warfighter recovering from very real wounds from combat needs spiritual healing and an acceptance of faith to truly heal. "You have to address the spirit side, whatever that is to you—faith and God is critical, critical in each of our individual healing."

A Hardened Heart

Tom grew up going to Lutheran school. "I was forced into it," he recalled, "so when you're forced into something and you're doing it, does that mean you are really doing it? But I did believe in God. When I went in the Army, I still believed in God, but He wasn't at the forefront of all that I thought about. I would pray every night before I went out on a mission. I would pray for my men, to keep them safe, for help to make the right decisions, bring everyone home. So I was still faithful."

But after a while, after fighting in combat and brutal missions over and over again, Tom began to lose many of the things he had held close to his heart. "You lose empathy and compassion toward other humans because you hate them," he shared. "Because you have to hate all of them to do the things you have to do. You dehumanize the enemy. So it's easier to do what you have to do. But the moral injury comes later, after you do what you have to do after you redeploy. And when you come home again, you are sick, and you're no longer seemingly under threat. That was when I was sitting down and started thinking about all the things I've done. And I would have stayed there if it hadn't been for Jen. And I had Jen suggesting that there were answers to my questions."

Reading the Bible for the first time helped ease the burden Tom was carrying. War was present throughout. "I didn't read the Bible. I'm a guy that likes facts. And if you told me something, I would challenge everything you said: *Where'd you get that? Who*

said that? Are they crazy? I'd interrogate statements because everything we know, we've been taught by somebody who was taught by somebody, and so on down the line. I started reading the Bible cover to cover, to actually read this thing instead of listening to other people telling me about it. And I'm halfway through First Samuel and it's been nothing but war. Nothing but slaughtering people just because they're bad. Just killing other people so their people could pass through. I'm thinking, *Wow, okay, that lightens the load a little bit. I wasn't murdering.*"

Morally Injured

The biggest challenge for Tom, the heaviest burden he was carrying, was the moral injury he suffered. The demands of his job were brutal, raw, and very real. He felt he had become the monster. "I certainly never thought of moral injury as a man in war. I never thought of anything," Tom said. "I did my job, I was robotic. You train so hard so that you don't have to think. If you pause and think, you might end up dead. If you see that there's something in a person's hand, you ask, is it a weapon? If it is, you're dead, and I'm on to the next person. I couldn't think about who was that? How old were they? Female? Male? They had a weapon and they died. That was the job. And then you go to the next room, and you do that five times a night. And then every night for ninety days."

The hard part was afterward. After the job, after the violence. It was the pause that was so damaging to Tom. "Then you get a break. And then you, yourself, become the monster that you have to attack," he said. "You have to be a monster to fight a monster sometimes. And when all that stops, the moral injury symptoms kick in. *I hate everybody. I hate everything. I hate myself.* So how can I like anybody else?" Tom was sucked into a black hole, remaining there until he started to heal.

The healing was slow and grueling. "I couldn't do it with an unclear head. I had to tackle anger. I had to tackle alcohol. You have to tackle that thing that is the number one distraction or destructor in your life, whatever is consuming you, before you can get back to God," Tom said. It is not always simple. The hardest part, but the most crucial, is self-forgiveness.

"Because they're struggling over here, back home, it's not enough to tell somebody just ask God, pray to God. That's not going to do it for them because they are such a disbeliever," Tom explained. "Because their life is a living hell, from the time that they enlisted, volunteered, and now they hate themselves for volunteering for what they did."

Tom felt that everything was his fault, and he couldn't forgive himself for any of it. And when you can't forgive yourself, you can't forgive anybody. "Jen said to me one time, 'If Jesus can forgive, why can't you? Why can't you forgive yourself or other people?'" he recalled. "And that really struck me, like, why am I the holdout here? Why am I the guy that doesn't forgive people, when Jesus does it? Even God did. God forgave Moses." He could forgive Tom too. And Tom was learning to forgive himself, through the love of Christ.

Outward Symptoms

The Army did not classify Tom as having PTS or a traumatic brain injury that would alter his behavior, which added a daunting challenge to recognition and recovery. Back in 2013, the Army didn't want to check the PTS box since that would diminish his fitness-to-perform rating. (Thankfully, in the decade-plus since then, the "man up, shut up, put up, rub dirt on it" mentality, as Jen put it, within the Army has started to change.)

But there was indeed injury, and there were symptoms. Tom was taking sixteen different medications, sleeping no more than two hours a night, overconsuming alcohol as a form of self-medication, and had intense rage. They fought often. Once a month Jen would see him banging a gun against the side of his head, begging her to let him go through with it.

The pain for them both was excruciating.

He was never truly present. "We would be on a date. I'd have to practically snap my fingers, and sometimes actually did, and say to him, 'I'm over here.' I wondered if he was actually hearing me. His head was on a swivel. He'd look one way, then another. He wasn't there with me in a restaurant, a bar, a park. He was in Iraq or Africa.

"It got to the point that I once said to him that we would not go out to eat unless he was okay with sitting with his back to the entrance. And do you know what he told me when I asked him to do that one thing? 'No,' he said, 'there's no way I will ever do that.'

"We would be driving down the street and switching lanes. And I'm like, 'What are you doing?' Like there's no cars even around. He'd say, 'When you go under an underpass, you go in on this lane, but you always come out on the other one.' I'd stare at him. 'We're in St. Louis. Dude, there's nobody standing on an overpass with an AK.'"

Tom was angry and grief-stricken, and with good reason. "He would talk about Black Hawk Down. Why did Gary get taken? Why did Randy? These young men losing their lives at this really young age. It isn't fair!" But she noticed an additional quality: "Even at that time, it seemed like Tom had a victim mindset."

But it wasn't just his behaviors that needed addressing. Tom had very real physical injuries, below the surface.

Physical Internal Injury

A visit to a brain injury specialist revealed crucial answers. Tom's brain had sustained verifiable, significant damage. The specialist told them Tom's brain was in worse condition than what the doctor had seen in a pro football player who had played for twenty seasons.

He went on to list what he expected were Tom's symptoms. Sleeplessness. (Check.) Rage. (Check.) You say things that you don't mean to say. (Check.) The list went on. Jen sat stunned, partially relieved and partially still worried. She had some answers to questions about why her husband acted the way that he did. The parts of his brain that regulated sleep and regulated emotion were damaged. Most relieving of all, the doctor said that he could fix Tom's PTS with over-the-counter supplements.

At least now they understood that Tom was injured, as if he had a broken arm or a broken leg that would heal. That was so important to them and is one of the foundational principles they apply in their nonprofit.

"We used to say that PTS is one of the invisible wounds of war," Jen said. "We don't do that anymore. PTS is *visible*. It shows up on brain scans. You can beat it, and so our new tagline is, 'Where the war within is won.' And PTS shows up in the very same ways regardless of the cause. Tom and I had the same PTS symptoms. Mine came from childhood abuse and sexual assault. His came from combat. But our behavior and the ways our brains were damaged were the same."

The Transformative Power of Prayer

Once Jen and Tom had stepped back into faith, they started to pray. The power of prayer had a transformative effect on Jen's and Tom's healing. In their darkest moments and most frightening times, calling on God brought peace and the knowledge they were not in this alone. Without God, it seemed—and was—impossible.

"When I started praying and opening myself up in those times when Tom and I would have the most horrific fight or maybe I just saw Tom put a gun to his head and beg me to allow him to take his life, the only person I could go to in those times is Jesus and to God," Jen shared. "When I didn't have them to go to, when it was just me fighting Tom's demons, it felt impossible. It felt bigger than me; I felt like I was gonna lose. My one hundred percent take on this battle was that it was going to take my life in one way or another."

The more Jen prayed, the more she felt God and His comfort. "When I started surrendering and allowing God into my life, praying to Jesus every day, in those moments where we would fight or something would happen I would turn to Jesus and I would feel this peace. I would feel like I wasn't alone. Because so much of my journey without Him was lonely. It was so lonely."

The prayer helped with the fear too. "Everything in my life was fear, fear, fear. What if this, what if that, consumed me. That doesn't happen anymore. Because as soon as those voices start, I say to myself, *that's not God, that's not Jesus.*"

A deep peace started to come forward, within Jen and within their relationship. "The more I prayed, and the more I started to ask Jesus to come into my life, the more I felt Him when things would get tough," Jen said. "I would call Jesus out loud, on my knees, hands in the air, saying, *I need you to help me with this, please, please, please.* And a peace and calm would fall over Tom, or he would come in the other room sometimes after prayer to apologize—instead of that taking Tom two or three days to do that, it would be five minutes.

"And I know it was Jesus working. And after Tom started accepting Jesus, we would still argue, but I could tell Tom had empathy and compassion when it wasn't there before. And that's Jesus."

Tom had been in such a dark place. But prayer worked for him—and so did trusting Jesus. "I was a monster. I hated myself. I hated everything. I loved her," Tom said. "I think that the dark side had me and I took the easy path he was leading me down."

When Tom's prayers started working, he thought, "Maybe there's something to this—maybe it's a coincidence. Maybe it's just me thinking differently." The more he was internally saying kinder things to himself, and praying to *feel* forgiven, the better he kept getting.

"Self-forgiveness allowed me to love myself through Jesus, which in turn allowed me to appreciate and love other people," Tom shared. "I had to get rid of that monster. I had to stop listening to his voice. And it's an ongoing struggle: Jesus forgives me/I'm not worthy of forgiveness. That's the voice. That's the tension, that's the dark side trying to pull me over."

It was somehow easy for Tom to believe the negative voice without question, but so hard for him initially to believe anything positive. So Tom prayed. "And I do that all the time now, especially when things first start," he described. "If I can catch my anger quick enough, it doesn't get out of control, because it will get out of control at times. Stopping and praying makes it easier to walk away and give space. I've learned that it's okay to sit there by yourself and just talk to God and listen and wait. And that other voice will come back, it will likely always come back, but I have the tools now to better deal with it."

"And putting that gun to my head? I never wanted to do it," said Tom. "I was just doing it. That was the confusing part back then. I'd ask myself, *Why am I doing this? It's not me doing this*. But you can't tell somebody that! Of course, they'd think it *is* you doing it. I never put a bullet in it. I would never do that. That's not what I've been taught."

After Tom learned his brain was physically injured, he felt relief. "This is not just me thinking things. My brain is physically causing me to do stuff I don't want to do," he said. "And at that point, when I learned that, I had to start listening and start being more attentive and start praying more."

Bringing Peace to Christmas

Of particular difficulty for Tom and Jen were holidays and special occasions. Tom admits that he ruined many Christmases. As he's turned to Christ, he's been better able and willing to express what he wasn't able to articulate before: "I can't access the type of joy I see other people having at those times. I'd see the kids, I'd see Jen, and they are so happy, and I'm jealous. I'm resentful. Why can't I have that?"

Tom's responses and reactions weren't uncommon. The All Secure crisis hotline is far busier during the Christmas season than at any other. But for the Satterlys, Christmas improved when they centered the holiday on Christ.

Tom's complicated feelings involved survivor's guilt and a disgust at materialism, and the cycle of guilt over his behavior. "It was really hard for me to be sitting around and opening presents. And so much of Christmas was that," Tom said. "And a lot of survivor guilt shows up at that time. Combine that with gifts, and it's hard. Somebody gets a Nintendo and you're thinking about all your buddies who are all dead. And I get it—maybe I shouldn't be that way. So, then there's that guilt too."

But this past Christmas was different. "Jesus was, intentionally, a bigger part our celebration," said Jen. "I found a portrait of the baby Jesus and put that up in our living room. We had a manger beneath the tree. We engaged in a lot of prayer and me talking with the kids about this is the time when we celebrate the birth of the Savior. So if we're buying presents, it should be for others. It should be about giving. We are honoring Jesus, and anything else that happens is like gravy. That took a lot of the pressure off of us."

Jen released pressure off herself too. "Like a lot of people, I wanted Christmas to be perfect. I'd do everything I could to make it that way. And it's never been and never will be perfect. In the past that would really upset me. So now, I think, it doesn't have to be perfect, it has to be decent. It has to have the right focus and not the right gift or not the right food. It's okay to have an okay day."

One Savior

Another part of the Satterlys' healing process was the recognition of a specific type of pressure Jen had been feeling, not uncommon in combat veteran spouses. "I felt a lot of pressure for years. Tom used to say all the time, '*You saved me,*' or call me his 'savior,'" Jen said. "And I never liked how he expressed that because we have one Savior. I felt I almost had this Jesus-like expectation of me being Tom's savior. He would say, 'I would be dead without you, I would never be here without you. You saved my life.' Yes, those things are true, but to be the spouse on the receiving end of that is hard. Because those statements are also *not* true.

"I'm not your savior. Jesus is your Savior," Jen said. "I'm human. I felt a lot of pressure to fix Tom, to heal him, to get him mentally right, physically right, spiritually right."

Since Tom would look to Jen for answers, Jen felt like she could never quite keep up with his healing, because it wasn't coming internally through God. "It was coming through all of these outside Band-Aids and fixes," she said.

That pressure very often falls upon the spouse. At the All Secure Foundation, Jen would have countless spouses calling her saying, *I'm the therapist, and the physical therapist, and the doctor, and the spiritual leader, and nobody's taught me to be any of these roles, yet they've been assigned to me.* "I definitely felt the role of savior meant I had to be all things to him," Jen said. "That can feel so heavy. I told Tom, 'I hate that you called me your savior, because that means I can also fail you. I hate that you say I've saved your life, because that means I can mess up some time and be the cause of you taking your life. I don't want that. I don't want that responsibility for your life. *You* have to be responsible for your life."

But when Tom found God, the pressure on Jen was extinguished. "Now that he knows who the true Savior is, the relationship shifted," Jen shared. "Howard Storm used this analogy: When someone is struggling and lost at sea, like so many PTS sufferers are, be a lighthouse. You don't have to jump into the water and try to swim out and rescue him. You could drown. You need to be there on the shore. Flip the switch and turn on the lighthouse beacon.

"And when that switch flipped for us, when Jesus started showing up over and over again in so many ways, our house feels different."

*   *   *

The Satterlys are a stunning example of how the peace of Jesus can be transformative. The enemy tried hard to keep them from where they were going: proclaiming Jesus as the Lord and Savior, sharing their faith with the warfighter community and the world, bringing healing to so many. But the Lord was always near; and as the Satterlys released anxiety and fear and accepted Jesus, praying to God with all their requests, the peace of God flooded their hearts and minds in Christ Jesus, and they knew God was with them every step of the way.

They are living testaments that with God, all things are possible. Declaring that in their home they serve the Lord helped shatter the insidious PTS cycles of pain and anguish, toxic behavior, and misplaced worship that had snared them for years. It's a continued effort, a marathon of epic proportions—but with God they are a majority against all enemies brought home from war.

Now fearless warriors in Christ's army, they serve as an all-secure lighthouse for us all.

The Lord will fight for you, and you shall hold your peace.

—EXODUS 14:14

TEAM C: Raiderettes Tiphanie, Emily, Ashlee, Meena, and Cole with two soldiers just back from a patrol at a FOB in Iraq, 2009.

Army strong! Pretty sure us cutting up our
Army T-shirts into "cute tops" wasn't regulation . . .
Iraq, 2009.

Former State
Department
spokesperson and
current Naval
Reservist Morgan
Ortagus.

Morgan posing at the wheel of a US Army vehicle
in Baghdad, 2007.

16

Bold in Faith

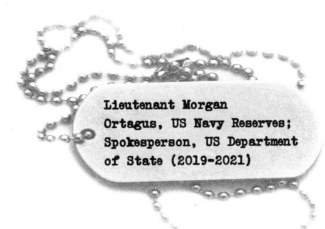

Lieutenant Morgan Ortagus, US Navy Reserves; Spokesperson, US Department of State (2019-2021)

While Morgan Ortagus was serving as US State Department spokesperson in the Trump administration in 2020, the world learned of the acts of genocide being committed by the Chinese Communist Party against the minority Muslim Uighurs. The CCP was using forced sterilization and abortion methods, injecting pregnant women and forcing them to take pills to miscarry the babies.

Morgan was six months pregnant with her first child at the time. She felt deep empathy for these Uighur women half the world away. The State Department released a series of videos where Morgan spoke out against these horrific sterilization and abortion camps. Her hope was that the visual of an American pregnant woman in a senior administration official role speaking up for them, about them, and in support of them would give the Uighur women hope.

At the time, Morgan was thirty-seven, working half the month at the State Department and half the month traveling internationally. It was beyond busy and chaotic—but yet it was that precise moment that she was visibly pregnant, in a position with a microphone on the world's stage, calling attention to the atrocities being committed against a minority population and showing the Uighur women they were seen and supported.

A pregnant, Jewish woman speaking out against human rights abuses, echoing what had happened in the Holocaust. It is a crucial, fundamental part of Jewish faith and teachings: stepping up and speaking out for the oppressed and the hopeless.

For Morgan, it all started with a very special first night of Hanukkah, in one of Saddam Hussein's palaces in Iraq.

A Full Circle of Faith

During the 2007 Iraq surge, Morgan was on a temporary duty assignment from the State Department, charged with assisting the US Agency for International Development (USAID) in Baghdad. It was a rough time in the war; the coalition-controlled Green Zone in central Baghdad was still being targeted intermittently. Morgan loved the work and the people, but peace and security certainly were not guaranteed.

Morgan's then-boyfriend, now husband, is Jewish, and Morgan was in the middle of discovering Judaism. Morgan had been attending Friday night Shabbat services, the Jewish Sabbath. It felt right, to be faithful while in the war zone. At the time, the new US embassy wasn't built, so the weekly Shabbat and any holiday services were held in different buildings throughout the Green Zone.

That year, Hanukkah began on December 4. The first night's service was held in one of Saddam Hussein's palaces. "It was an amazing experience," Morgan told me. Hanukkah, celebrated for eight nights, always begins on the twenty-fifth of the Hebrew month of Kislev. Because the Jewish calendar is lunisolar (based on both the moon and the sun), the date of Hanukkah shifts relative to dates on the Gregorian calendar. How the date of Hanukkah aligns with Christmas varies, but both are often around the same time of year; sometimes they even overlap.

Hanukkah is a Hebrew word meaning "dedication." The holiday of Hanukkah, also known as the "festival of lights," celebrates the rededication of the Holy Temple in Jerusalem. In 168 BCE, the Seleucid king Antiochus IV Epiphanes sent soldiers to Jerusalem. They brutally ruled the Holy Land, outlawed Jewish observances, and desecrated the Temple, setting it up for the worship of Greek gods. Jews were told to convert—or die.

A menorah American personnel placed in Saddam Hussein's palace in Baghdad for a Hanukkah celebration.

The Jewish people resisted. The military resistance was coordinated by the Maccabee family, with Judah Maccabee leading the way. Though vastly outnumbered, and facing one of the most skilled and powerful armies around, the small band of Jews not only won the battle but drove their oppressors out of the land and rededicated the Temple.

Then a miracle occurred. The Hellenistic Syrians had contaminated much of the oil that was used to fuel lamps. The Jews wanted to light the menorah—a candelabrum—in the newly freed Temple. They poured what oil they could find into the menorah, expecting it to last only one day. To their amazement, it lasted eight days. The holiday is now celebrated for that length of time in recognition of the miracle of the oil that lasted, and of the light it created.

Of note, the Maccabees were one of those biblical groups about whom others have spoken in this book. They were fierce freedom fighters who waged ferocious battle. The name Maccabee is an acronym for the Hebrew words, "Who is like You among all the powers, God?" Judah and his band of brothers—four of them—helped win the battle that is celebrated at Hanukkah. Death and violence, war and subsequent peace, are heavily present throughout the Bible.

Thus, when Morgan and the others lit the menorah that night in Baghdad, in a place marked by much oppression, in a palace built by a sadistic tyrant but taken over by peacekeepers, both history and prayers echoed down the halls. Starting with the ceremonial lighting of the first (center) candle, on each night of Hanukkah celebrants say prayers in Hebrew as they kindle the holiday lights. On the very first night of Hanukkah each year, a poignant prayer is added.

Translated into English:

Blessed are You, Lord our God, King of the universe, who has kept us
alive, sustained us, and enabled us to reach this occasion.

It is particularly meaningful to God's chosen people during this holiday that indeed His protection has enabled them to celebrate and to worship in that moment, in that time. The relationship between the Jewish people and Gentiles is one of steadfast, biblically commanded support. Psalm 122:6 commands believers to pray for the peace of Jerusalem, to seek prosperity and good for the Jewish people. As such, it was fitting one of the attendees that night was a US soldier who was Christian and whose father back home in Arkansas had built and shipped over a stainless-steel menorah for the group to use. What a remarkable, and biblical, first Hanukkah for Morgan.

"It's easy to be dismissive of religion when you're in a safe place like America," Morgan shared. "But then, all of a sudden, you feel everybody's lives are on the line, and you're in a war zone, so you start to feel a little bit more differently about faith." This was particularly pronounced for Morgan as well while she began her conversion process and continued her tours of duty for the United States.

She had started the conversion process in Washington, DC, by taking in-person classes. As she progressed, being assigned by the Treasury Department to the US embassy in Riyadh, Saudi Arabia, complicated things. Fortunately, technology enabled her to Skype with a rabbi every Friday. She was especially pleased to share in person important Jewish holidays with friends of different religious beliefs. After her first Hanukkah in Baghdad and her rigorous studies in Saudi Arabia, she held her conversion ceremony back home in the United States. A full circle of faith.

The Abraham Accords

Morgan found her faith under the "most extreme, most odd, most challenging circumstances," but she considers it perhaps a sign: "My destiny was to have the strength and the conviction and the calling to stand up and speak out on these issues." This destiny included being one of a very small team of Trump administration officials who worked on the historic Abraham Accords—a series of bilateral peace and normalization agreements between Israel and the United Arab Emirates, Bahrain, Sudan, and Morocco—alongside Secretary of State Michael Pompeo and Jared Kushner, Senior Advisor to President Trump.

They were making peace between Israel and Arab states. It was unheard of, and they made history. "Working on the Abraham Accords really closed the full circle of my faith for me," Morgan shared. "It was just so historic, and I was pregnant with my own Jewish daughter, while being a part of that."

Being bold in faith and for faith was crucial for the success of those peace accords. "In every generation, someone is trying to kill off the Jews," Morgan said. "During the Abraham Accords, people in government and elsewhere thought we were crazy. *It's hopeless. Peace between the Israelis and the Arabs can't happen.* That's when you have to be the most bold. And as a member of a faith that's targeted around the world and here at home, you have two choices: fight or flight. You can hide your faith, or you can boldly put it on display."

Many critics at the time argued there could be no Israeli-Arab peace agreement without first achieving Israeli Palestinian peace. Many cynics decried the administration for even attempting a historic peace. But Morgan stayed strong in her boldness, and strong in her faith in the face of the opposition and criticism. "There's a common theme among the Abrahamic faiths that you have to believe that you are called for a higher purpose, for higher meaning," she explained. "We couldn't let fear of failure stop us from trying something new."

The Biggest Star of David

Even after helping to achieve historic peace between the Jewish state and neighboring Arab states, her boldness in her faith was tested. Immediately before one of her first trips to Germany with Secretary of State Pompeo, the media had been suggesting that people not overtly display any Jewish symbols. Antisemitism had been festering in Europe and was at an especially alarming level. "The media's advice was to hide your faith, hide your Judaism," Morgan told me. "And I just thought that was horrific. I couldn't believe that. So I wore the biggest Star of David necklace that I could find."

Morgan refuses to hide her faith in the face of adversity. "It's my faith that made me bolder," she said. Every generation of Jews has faced persecution, prosecution, and punishment of all kinds. For the most part, Jews have found a safe haven and refuge in America. But none of that security is certain, none of it guaranteed, as current events continue to remind us."

"Wherever you are in the world, whether you're Christian, Jewish, Muslim, there's a place in the world where people of your faith are probably persecuted," Morgan said. "And your choice is to hide who you are, and hide what you believe, or to be bold and be loud, to be unapologetic." Morgan acknowledges the convenience and luxury of living in America and living in Tennessee, where people are incredibly supportive. "But there are Jews in Los Angeles and New York City today who have to think twice about their own safety. It's crazy to me that we talk about this in the context of the United States of America, because these are the fights I've been having in national security for the last twenty years around the world. And the fact that we're having them here is pretty dour."

Especially in the current climate where global antisemitism and violence against Israel and Jews has reached a fever pitch, it's important to lean on faith. "If you're Christian, Jewish, Muslim, you have to have faith during those dark hours. Otherwise, how can you get through them? I also think that whenever the world looks especially dour, I do remember that doesn't have to be the story. The ending isn't prewritten other than how the Bible says what the end of days will be like. In between now and then, we have a lot of control, a lot of say, about how this works out for America. So, what we do for Israel, the Middle East, isn't prewritten either. We still can very much control our destiny. It's important to remember that not that long ago, we were making peace between Israel and those Arab states. I'm still hopeful that it can happen again."

For the LORD God is a sun and shield: the LORD will give grace and glory: no good thing will He withhold from them that walk uprightly.

—PSALM 84:11

Repairing the World

In addition to working in various capacities in national security, Morgan is also an officer in the US Navy Reserves. Not only does she see the bigger global picture through her work in the intelligence community, but she's helped shape national defense policy as well as develop international treaties. So many of the individuals in this book have talked about doing their duty, following orders, and faithfully defending the United States. Morgan has been in rooms and at tables where the policy and intelligence informs what these brave men and women have been sent out to do. She may also end up, as a reservist, executing those missions herself.

One of the central principles of Jewish faith is *tikkun olam*, which means "repairing the world." Jews should engage in various forms of action in order to improve the world, to make it more fair and just. As a person of Jewish faith, you are responsible for your own welfare, and that of the larger world's welfare too.

"Whenever you're representing the United States of America, you have to show the world that you have faith," Morgan said. "America sets the example for the rest of the world. We are very diverse here, and, for the most part, we get along. Jews and Christians, what underpins our faith is the same belief that we are called to a higher purpose, that we are all called to do things on this earth. You believe that you're fulfilling what God called you to do, and then you're able to do incredible things."

Morgan is an incredibly strong individual, not usually very emotive. But the vicious, catastrophic attack on Israel by the terror group Hamas on October 7, 2023, left a global—and personal—impact. "Since October 7, I've felt very broken," Morgan shared. "I think that's because I'd worked on these issues overseas, and then to see what's also gone on here in the US broke my heart."

We were on live television together shortly after October 7. Morgan was sitting next to me and she became overcome with emotion. "I remember vividly sitting on the set of your show, right next to you, and watching a plane of Israelis or Jews that had landed. Crowds ran up to that aircraft and it seemed as if they wanted to hijack that plane and get at those Jews. I guess they wanted to beat them to death," she said. "And all of this, so many of these things, made me feel the way that I did after 9/11. And to think that on October 7, more Jews were killed in one day than since the Holocaust. And maybe— like then on 9/11 when so many of us were snapped back or freshly snapped into a harsh reality—maybe Jews in America have been lulled to sleep. We became complacent; everything was easy and safe for us here. And then to be reminded that anywhere in the world antisemitism is alive, is rising, we have to stand against that. Prayer is very private to me. But after October 7, I now stand up and demonstrate my pride in my faith."

*   *   *

Morgan's boldness in her faith has shaped world history. It helped drive the momentum for the historic Abraham Accords, bringing peace between Israel and Arab states, leaving a permanent positive imprint on the chosen people. Her unapologetic proclaiming of her Jewish faith has sent strong messages to allies and foes alike, that she will not hide her faith in the face of antisemitism, and that in representing America abroad she represents unrestrained freedom to worship and an intolerance of persecution.

And her solidarity with the Muslim Uighurs on the global stage as a senior administration official messaged to the oppressed and the oppressors that she, an American Jewish woman with a Jewish daughter, will not stand by silent during a genocide. From a meaningful conversion to Judaism that saw her celebrate her first Hanukkah in one of Saddam Hussein's palaces in Baghdad to Shabbat in Saudi Arabia to the final ceremony in the United States, her faith journey was a full, special circle.

The Lord has commanded us to be bold, strong, and courageous, for He is always with us, and will neither fail nor abandon us. Morgan is living this command every day, fulfilling God's noble purpose for her life. She is demonstrating to the world that she will never fail in her endeavors to make the world more fair and just, nor abandon the Jewish people or anyone suffering at the hands of oppressors. With her boldness, she is inspiring millions and defending millions. Repairing the world indeed.

The wicked flee though no one pursues,
but the righteous are as bold as a lion.

—PROVERBS 28:1

AFTERWORD

It has been my utmost honor to serve as a messenger for the profound stories of the warriors within this book. I remain greatly impacted and forever inspired by their reverent experiences with God and their deeply personal experiences with faith on the battlefield. That they have trusted me with their stories is humbling. The common thread throughout their compelling perspectives is that God is always with us, without fail, without exception. It is His hand that guides our way, it is His comfort we feel, it is His wings under which we take refuge.

These American heroes remind us how multifaceted service is; how honorable and exceptional our warriors are; how utterly and selflessly they—and their families—fulfill duty. How many forms battles and sacrifice take, on how many fronts combat takes place. How complicated and traumatic and tragic war is, how great the loss of the Ultimate Sacrifice.

Their breathtaking accounts remind us how simple and magnificent God's love is for us; how transformative it is when we feel His love, when we accept His mercy, when we pray; and the life-changing—and lifesaving—effect of surrendering your life to Christ. Their stories remind us of the heavy burdens warriors carry, and of the only Savior that can lighten their load.

After each interview, we ended our time together praying in gratitude. It's fitting then, in these final pages, that I do the same now.

These are exceptional individuals. Each demonstrates a Christ-like capacity for putting the needs of others ahead of their own, of brotherhood before self, of service before all else. Their servant's hearts and lion's courage have blessed countless others on the front lines and on the home front, myself included.

With my whole heart of gratitude, thank you, God, for blessing me indeed, and for the opportunity to enlarge Your territory with these humble men and women, these soldiers for Christ. I pray, dear reader, that you, too, will be inspired and encouraged to proclaim your love for Jesus Christ, and your love for one another.

Let the peace of Christ rule in your hearts,
since as members of one body you were called to peace.

—COLOSSIANS 3:15

Memorial Day Soliloquy,
A Mother's Lament

(Attending Mass) Before the parade

The Sacrifice of the Mass for our departed comrades;
"Kyrie Eleison, Christe Eleison"
The Offertory; "Spare them O Lord";
Heads bowed.
The Consecration; "Take Ye and eat . . . Take Ye and drink."
My son this Mass is offered up to you . . .
My son's life and blood were given to the enemy.
But I must not think that way; it is blasphemous.
"God so loved the world that he gave His only begotten son."
My son also gave his life . . .
"God forgive me"; "An everlasting abode stands ready in Heaven."
"O Lord, I am not worthy."
Thank you dear Lord for allowing me to partake of you.
"Requiescat in Pace."

(Leaving the Church)

The silent tread of men, flags held high . . .

From the darkness to bright sunlight,

Flags waving in the breeze,

The ruffle of drums, the blare of the horns,

The sound of music, the shuffling of feet.

As each man and woman takes a firm step forward in the line of march

Their thoughts keep in time with the cadence,

ONE, TWO, THREE, FOUR,

"He did it for us."

"He would be proud."

"Hail Mary, full of Grace . . ."

Each person has his own image of the Sacrificial Lamb.

People watching, memories of their own.

Wars repeat, times change, but

Endearing thoughts in each one's mind and the emotions of the heart

Never change.

And there arises a prayer on their lips,

"Requiescat in Pace" for those who died that other men may live.

May they rest in peace.—

LT. LUELLA LORENZ COCHRAN DAVIS,

US ARMY NURSE CORPS, WHOSE BROTHER JOSEPH LORENZ

DIED IN FRANCE IN WORLD WAR I.

MAY 1962.

ACKNOWLEDGMENTS

With my whole heart of gratitude, thank you:

First and foremost, to the extraordinary warriors whose voices make up this book. I pray I have honored your stories and your service.

Col. Tim Karcher, Maj. Jeff Struecker, Sgt. Jeremiah Wilber, Lt. Col. Anthony Randall, Lt. Cdr. Chris and Lt. Cdr. Angie Baker, SFC Jessica Harris, Col. Doug Collins, Capt. Charlie Plumb, SMA Darryle Endfinger, Col. Tom Moe, Cpl. Howard Spurlock, MSgt. Robert Burr, Sgt. Andy Negra, LT Luella Lorenz Cochran, CCStd. Anton Lorenz, Sarah Verardo, Laura De Roo, CSM Tom Satterly and Jen Satterly, and Lt. Morgan Ortagus, it was my honor to serve as a messenger for your faith. Writing this book will remain a privilege of my life.

To Gary Brozek and Jennings Grant, for this journey of a lifetime. This book would not exist without either of your indescribable contributions, and I could not have chosen better wingmen.

To the esteemed leadership at Fox News, I am impressed and inspired every day by the elite caliber and the support of those at the helm. It's a dream come true every day, and I am profoundly grateful: Suzanne Scott, Jay Wallace, Lauren Petterson, Dianne Brandi, Megan Albano, Gavin Hadden, Kim Rosenberg, Tom Lowell, Jill Van Why, Meade Cooper, Megan Clarke, John Sylvester, Maria Donovan, Jon Glenn, Porter Berry, and Melissa Barette.

To my incredible *Outnumbered* show cohosts and team, you are priceless. My sisters in Christ and on set, Kayleigh McEnany and Harris Faulkner. To the phenomenal *Fox True Crime Podcast* team, you are irreplaceable. Also, the husband did it. To Fox Nation, thank you for being the platform for my passions.

Thank you to the molecule of awesome that is the entire heart of Fox—all those creative, talented, brilliant, hilarious, dynamic, wonderful souls that make up the Fox family. You are what makes Fox so special, and it's impossible to describe what a delight it all is. Thank you for including me in your show families and Secret Santas and letting me seagull your food. I laugh and learn every day from a dorm room with a miniature car and roller skates in it. I can't imagine anything better.

All you impressive talent setting the example for me every day: Ainsley, Brian, Steve, and Lawrence; Carley and Todd; Dana and Bill; Sandra and John; Martha; Neil; The Five; Bret; Laura; Jesse; Sean; Greg; Trace (you are why I'm here!); Pete, Rachel, and Will; Rick and Adam; dear Shannon and Sami; Kat and Tyrus; Johnny Belisario (totally!), Tommy O'Connor, Elle Penner, James Coffey, Arash Mosaleh, Gene Nelson, Joan McNaughton, Paul Mauro, Chrystie Del Corso,

Gabby Valenti, Joe DeVito, Mike Castillo, Andre Confuorto, Ryan Brosky, Joe Machi, Dan Kendall, Caroline Sherwood, Viki Ristanovic, Remy Numa, Nicole Knee Cooper, Julia Walsh, Alexa Mancini, Kimberly Pitz, Lexi Hall, Ilana Berman, Audrey Pooley, Jason Kopp, Brian Tully, Michael LaMarca, Kelly May, Max Kiviat, Kristy Cappiello, Mario Goncalves, Brian Paz, Nick Di Brita, Scott Sanders, Joey Muniz, Maria Louka, Anthony Rocchio, Brett Zoeller, Amy Fenton, Sean O'Rourke, Christina Trupia, Mina Pertesis, Henry O'Shea, Stefanie Hall, Roman Colfini, Montana Marsilio, Brooke Jaffe, Sabrina Wolman, Stephanie Woloshin, Alyssa Carey, Rachel Rea, Sara Sonnack, Kelly Nish, Jon Sampson, Kevin Pinckney, Lucky Punturieri, Evans Manuel, Goose Borujow, Daniel Darline, Jim Gorman, sweet Katherine Horsford, Devon Kelly, Jason Bonewald, Matt Pascarella, Mikey Addvensky, Josh Harman, Kimberly Capasso, and Kaitlynn Wall, I am so grateful for and to you.

Jimmy, it's all magic, my dearest friend. Jenny, Linc, Dean, and Tess, meet you in the backyard.

Kennedy, Dagen McDowell, Dina Tamburino, Alexis McAdams, there is not enough prosecco in the world to toast properly to our friendship and my love for you.

To Cameron LeSiege and Christina, the beauty you create and the grace you maintain is otherworldly. I love you both.

Manny Rios, Jenna Pizzuta, and Allie Franz, we are flowers in a garden all because of you.

To Luke and Daniel and team UTA, my sanity is preserved for only one reason and that's you! Your support is invaluable, and I treasure our friendship. A thousand thank-yous.

To Lisa and the HarperCollins team, for the opportunity to proclaim my faith in Jesus Christ and to serve as a small messenger for these extraordinary warriors and their beautiful stories of faith. I remain deeply grateful to your outstanding team.

Thank you for the ironclad support, Media Relations. Thank you for all the care and protection and walks, Fox Security, NYPD, and NJSP. I was kidding about the radar detector.

To my precious in-laws, I couldn't have dreamed of a better bonus family.

To my family, you are my everything. Mom and Dad, Uncle Sal, Auntie Catherine, John and Joleen and the girls, Fran and A, Jody and the boys, Nancy, Dale, Bunny and John, Kristine and Bill, Barbie and Greg, Cindy, Mike and Kari, Jim and Giovanna, Mary Ann, Cousin Helene and Jenny and Bob and the girls, the entire Monterey family, Paul and Sandy, and all our dearly departed in heaven, whom I feel and miss every day. For the best sandwiches in the world, go to Cousin Bennett's deli in Monterey.

Team S! The light of my life. We'll have that BI compound and I can't wait.

Team Gerry! The adventures are far from over. Start packing (again). Fo'castle.

To my sisters, Compagno Girlz forever—and above all else. Don't stop believin'.

And finally, to my husband, with whom I am rooted firmly in the Lord and in laughter. God gave me you. My greatest gift.

CREDITS

Endpaper photography courtesy of the Compagno Family

ABOUT THE AUTHOR

EMILY COMPAGNO is the cohost of *Outnumbered* and the host of FOX News Audio's *The FOX True Crime Podcast with Emily Compagno*. Compagno is an accomplished criminal law attorney whose career includes serving as a federal managing attorney and acting director in a top ten agency. A former cheerleader and captain for the Oakland Raiderettes, Compagno was one of five NFL cheerleaders to visit US troops deployed throughout Iraq and Kuwait on a USO tour in 2009. While an undergraduate at the University of Washington, she was awarded the US Air Force Reserve Officer Training Corps' Cadet of the Quarter Award.

FIRST EDITION

Library of Congress Cataloging-in-Publication Data has been applied for.

ISBN 978-0-06-341763-2

24 25 26 27 28 LBC 5 4 3 2 1